RECONSTRUCTION
OF THE POET

ALSO BY ZBIGNIEW HERBERT

The Collected Prose: 1948–1998
The Collected Poems: 1956–1998
Report from the Besieged City and Other Poems
Selected Poems
Still Life with a Bridle
Elegy for the Departure
Mr Cogito
The King of the Ants
Barbarian in the Garden

Reconstruction of the Poet

UNCOLLECTED WORKS OF ZBIGNIEW HERBERT

ZBIGNIEW HERBERT

EDITED AND TRANSLATED BY
ALISSA VALLES

An Imprint of HarperCollins*Publishers*

HarperCollins books may be purchased for educational, business, or sales promotional use. For information, please email the Special Markets Department at SPsales@harpercollins.com.

Ecco® and HarperCollins® are trademarks of HarperCollins Publishers.

A hardcover edition of this book was published in 2024 by Ecco, an imprint of HarperCollins Publishers.

FIRST ECCO PAPERBACK EDITION PUBLISHED 2025

Designed by Jennifer Chung

Library of Congress Cataloging-in-Publication Data has been applied for.

ISBN 978-0-06-288320-9 (pbk.)

HB 11.11.2024

ACKNOWLEDGMENTS

My profound gratitude to Katarzyna Herbert and Marysia Dzieduszycka for their unflagging support. For suggestions, scholarship, and practical help, I also thank Sarah Chalfant, Henryk Citko, John Coetzee, Andrzej Franaszek, Irena Grudzińska Gross, Jacek Kopciński, Michael Krüger, Krystyna Krynicka, Ryszard Krynicki, Adam Michnik, Paweł Prochniak, Christopher Ricks, Barbara Toruńczyk, and Marek Zaleski.

CONTENTS

INTRODUCTION

I

Reconstruction of the Poet: the title refers to Homer, the Ur-poet of Europe, who in Zbigniew Herbert's short drama talks back at the dull curators of posterity who claim to construe his greatness. But this "reconstruction" is not simply a joke about scholars; it also refers to the challenge of the poet of Herbert's generation to face the reality of the postwar world. The play's point of departure in ancient Greece was one of the things that made Zbigniew Herbert stand out as a new poet in postwar Poland: after the devastation of the war in which his contemporaries had been slaughtered, and after the general loss of faith in traditional pillars of culture, he stubbornly returned to the sources of that culture to test what in it still held water. His "reconstruction of the poet" was a lifelong task, a valiant campaign to rebuild out of rubble a poetry that would both measure up to ancient models (even when it subjected them to radical criticism) and articulate fully the truth of the moral and political catastrophe of modern Europe. The child of a tragic country, he was sustained by the gravity of classical order and the grace of a vital sense of humor.

When Herbert was a young man, he was in the habit of phoning up editors of literary magazines and introducing himself as "Mr. Frącowiak, author of a thousand sonnets." We learn this from Wisława Szymborska, who met Herbert in the 1950s and was one of many to testify to the delight he took in putting on an antic disposition. Herbert had a taste for theater from early on: in the years immediately after the war, when he was living in Kraków and working toward an economics degree, he participated in a number of stage productions and at least for a time entertained the idea of pursuing a career in the theater. What came of this was not altogether nothing: there are recordings from almost every stage of his life as a poet that show his gift for powerful and nuanced performance of his own work and poems he loved by others. His rich baritone voice can still elucidate poems, even those by now familiar, with precise intonation and emotion, and expressive shifts of pace and rhythm.

That Herbert had a lasting and passionate engagement with both classical and contemporary theater is clear from the many reviews he devoted to theater productions over the years, and from the wide array of traditions reflected in his own plays, from Greek choral drama to Dylan Thomas, Beckett, and Pinter. The three plays in this book were all written in the 1950s, a period when Herbert was studying philosophy, trying his voice, and articulating his purpose in the face of the hardening of Stalinist rule in Poland, which brought along with it narrow programmatic prescriptions for the arts and stifling censorship. His thinking about and in the theater helped him move toward a poetics that could do justice to the drama of doubt and the anguish of the war's aftermath.

In "Hamlet on the Border of Silence," an essay written in 1951, Herbert writes of the prince's education: "To the bitter truth of man's transience was added the truth about smiling villains, triumphant criminals."* The essay makes a passionate argument against the view of Hamlet as "a man who could not make up his mind," the phrase used by Laurence Olivier in the opening to his 1948 film adaptation of the tragedy. This view of the character is embedded in the Polish verb "hamletyzować," "to Hamletize," or to hesitate to act or take a decision as a result of "thinking too much." Herbert argues that in order to plumb the true depths of Shakespeare's play, we need to imagine Hamlet's past, and that to fail to do so is to trivialize his torment. "If only commentators, instead of fantasizing about what is written, would reconstruct what is missing and must be completed by the effort of a faithful imagination." This is the principle applied to Homer in Herbert's play *Reconstruction of the Poet*.

Herbert draws particular attention to Hamlet's humanism as it comes up against the brutality of the court at Elsinore. A young man of Renaissance virtues suddenly bereft not only of a father but also of faith in the rational basis of the world imparted to him in the course of his recent studies abroad in Würtemberg. Herbert's own predicament as a young man whose classical gymnasium education in prewar Lwów (now Lviv) in no way prepared him for the catastrophe of 1939–1945 clearly informs this reading. Twenty years old at the war's end, Herbert had found himself with a heart full of horror and grief, bitterly watching his country after liberation from the Nazis be taken over by another set of ideological thugs. He saw the survivors of Polish wartime resistance slandered, imprisoned, and many of them murdered; mourning for the vast numbers of the dead was a public drama to be carefully managed from on high and performed in accordance with the official view on the real heroes of the war. Though it is clear that he later exaggerated his own direct involvement in resistance, Herbert's solidarity with the Pol-

---

* Zbigniew Herbert, *The Collected Prose: 1948–1998*, 573–82.

ish underground struggle was sincere, and his fierce will to remember and honor those who perished remained an important driving force throughout his life. His early poems ask how to live in a devastated, betrayed world in which neither reason nor virtue, loyalty nor courage guarantee a dignified life or death.

In his Hamlet essay, Herbert writes of Descartes that he "built himself a cozy little temporary morality" to weather the storms of reason ignited by doubt; in contrast, Hamlet's doubt is existential—"Religious, metaphysical, moral, not merely methodological":

> [Hamlet] thinks with his whole life and with his whole person. The fingers touching Yorick's skull are the beginning of reflection; in Hamlet's conversation with his mother, thought bleeds and weeps.
>
> What is sometimes interpreted as indecision, in the intellectual sphere as well, is in fact Hamlet's orientation toward the concrete, the thought form that is an immediate reaction to reality, a response to a situation. That is why the Prince's soliloquies, in which the dramatization of thought reaches its peak, are as thrilling as the action, if indeed not more engaging. They are woven so subtly of thought's material that you can listen to them with your eyes closed, even regretting that they are being spoken aloud.

Herbert's notion of "thinking thought" is borrowed from the French existentialist philosopher Gabriel Marcel's "la pensée pensante." In an important correspondence of the period, with the dramatist Jerzy Zawieyski, Herbert called it "dramatic thinking," an idea he associates with the figures of Pascal and Kierkegaard, but above all with Socrates. It is not surprising that his playwriting often took the form of the "Play for Voices," a form of drama well suited to conveying "thought's material."

In July 1952 Zbigniew Herbert wrote to the philosopher Henryk Elzenberg, who had been until recently his professor at the University of Toruń and remained his mentor. Herbert had sent Elzenberg his essay on Hamlet, and his letter now reports:

> I'm racked by literary obsessions. At one point I started writing
> a novel; I've been carrying two stories around for a year and
> even . . . but I won't tell you, it's a terrible embarrassment to
> attempt anything in the theater. The characters come to me in the
> night with faces like hanged men, with upturned eyes and fettered
> hands, stifled by silence. I have to let their blood from time to
> time, otherwise they will die without a trace or a memory and this
> way I can use their blood to write of them that they existed.*

The attempt to which Herbert refers was *The Philosophers' Cave*, which can be read as, among other things, an apology for his choice of poetry over philosophy. Elzenberg's nonconformist stance led in the Stalinist years to his own professional isolation and ultimately his exile from the academy, which made him an obvious model for Socrates. Remembering Elzenberg in a poem many years later, Herbert recalled: "You were surrounded by sophists and those who think with a hammer / Dialectical frauds parishioners of nothingness."† The poem conveys Herbert's lasting sense of guilt at his own abandonment of philosophical discipline. He had once put it severely enough in a letter giving an account to his master.

> I put to myself—in answer to your letter—the question of
> what I really look for in philosophy. The question is rather

---

* Translated from Zbigniew Herbert and Henryk Elzenberg, *Korespondencja, Zeszyty Literackie*, Warsaw, 2002.
† Zbigniew Herbert, "To Henryk Elzenberg on the Centennial of his Birth," *The Collected Poems: 1956–1998*, 467–68.

Faustian, and perhaps it would be more appropriate to ask what philosophy demands of me, what responsibilities the discipline lays upon me. The answer to the first, more my own version of the question, turns out to be extremely compromising. I look for emotion. Powerful intellectual emotion, painful tensions between reality and abstraction, yet another rending, yet another, deeper than personal, cause for sorrow. And in that subjective cloud, respectable truth and sublime measure are lost, so I'll never be a decent university philosopher. I prefer suffering philosophy to brooding on it like a hen. I would rather it be a fruitless struggle, a personal cause, something going against the order of life, than a profession.[*]

It is this idea of living in the agon of thought that prepared the ground for the birth a decade and a half later of the thinking man with the limp ("On Mr Cogito's Two Legs"), the pockmarked face ("Mr Cogito Studies His Face in the Mirror"), and the skeptical stance toward music, poetry, and any art that is not anonymous.

In a study of Herbert's dramatic writings, the Polish scholar Jacek Kopciński quotes in full a typewritten note, found in the poet's archive and addressed to future directors of *The Philosophers' Cave*:

The action takes place on three levels, or in three layers. The first and outermost, played out on the "proscenium," is the prologue and the choral intermedia. The second, or real action, happens in the interior stage. Socrates' monologues make up the base level of the play, its final, deepest layer.

In the prologue the chorus speak with oratorical exaggeration, whereas in the interludes their speech is colloquial and indifferent.

---

[*] Translated from *Korespondencja*.

The symmetry of the construction, i.e., the return to the same scenes, can be underlined by the use of repeated musical motifs.

I don't have any particular wishes and leave it all to the director's invention. I would only insist on one thing, namely that the play be acted in a dry, caustic manner, without romantic sighs or sing-song.[*]

Kopciński sees an analogy between the architectural levels in the play and Herbert's description in the essay "Among the Dorians" of the movement in a Doric temple from the exterior to the inner sanctum, a center which "is an enclosed, rectangular chamber—called *naos*—dark as a ship's hold. Once it accommodated a statue of the god with his thunderbolt at rest. It is a place for priests rather than worshippers, the distant echo of a subterranean cave."[†] The "cave" of Herbert's play thus connotes more than the famous metaphorical cave of Plato's *Republic* on whose walls can be seen the shadows of ultimate realities: it also stands for the real prison cell of the philosopher and for the inner space or stage where the drama of consciousness is played out, or rather where it is played, because—as the chorus at the very beginning of the play warns the audience—the author offers no answers or solutions, only a balanced (as critics noted, classically balanced) form for the uncertain battle between reason and unreason. In one of his Herbertian soliloquies, Socrates address Dionysus:

> Perhaps reason—as you claim—
> is an instinct unto death
> an echo of nothingness
> You have chased me into this cave

---

[*] Translated from J. Kopciński, *Nasłuchiwanie: Sztuki na głosy Zbigniewa Herberta* (Listening In: Zbigniew Herbert's Plays for Voices), Warsaw: Więź, 2008, p. 164.
[†] Herbert, *The Collected Prose: 1948–1998*, 19.

and surrounded me with a throng of characters
all carrying my name
that is your last temptation
O Tempter
They come and ask
Who is the true Socrates?
You want me to suffer vertigo
at the sight of my likenesses
and to save myself from madness
by falling to my knees before divine frivolity
and the sacred play of appearances
You have two nights Dionysus
to seduce me
I have two days
to learn endurance
and perhaps in the end
tearing off mask after mask
I will read my own face
with dying fingers.

Curtain.

———

Reconstruction of the Poet, a short drama for radio, was written in 1958 in Paris, during Herbert's first trip abroad. As Kopciński remarks, where *Philosophers' Cave* dramatized a choice between philosophy and poetry, *Reconstruction* asks: "What kind of poetry?" In the play, the figure of Homer is conceived in direct opposition to the poet of Greek philology—Homer's voice cuts off the Professor, and the drama that he sets in motion brushes aside questions of historical authenticity in order to render a conflict at the heart of poetry itself. The two figures referred to (and contrasted) by the

Professor as Anonymous of Miletus and Anonymous of Milo turn out to be the same poet, and poetry a powerful force oscillating on an axis between the epic eye and the eye of the pebble. Again, the action moves from an outer layer of "common knowledge" (the scholar's banalities are placed on roughly the same level as the gossip of the chorus in *Philosophers' Cave*, the guesses of researchers on a level not much higher than a dice game), through a dialogue of Homer with his immediate environment, to an intimate reckoning with his task in Homer himself. It culminates in a rejection of the epic in favor of a poetry of the concrete, faithful to individual sense experience. This play follows in its general lines the argument of Herbert's early poetry, in which the epic modes of Romantic poets must yield to a tentative exploration of the world through the senses, above touch and sight, and mythical frameworks are subjected to a playful critique in which a traditional story is tested and corrected by new narrative angles.

The Other Room is also a short drama written for radio, with a very different setting: the cramped reality of postwar housing in People's Poland is the field where the deep tensions between generations, the effects of long deprivation and brutal political oppression, play out. If Herbert's first two plays reach back in time for the mythological sources that might bring spiritual or moral renewal, his third is diagnostic, stepping back to view more clearly what is out of joint in the present. Though it shows clearly the influence of the theater of the absurd, of Beckett and Ionesco, and of the Polish playwright Sławomir Mrożek, what is particularly Herbertian is its emphasis on *seeing* as a moral source. The object of the anonymous young couple's emotion and attention, the elderly lady who occupies the "other room" (in the Dramatis Personae she is no more than "what's on the other side of the wall") is never actually understood (from the dialogue) to be *seen*, and the play's first words, spoken by "SHE" are: "I can't look at her." Toward the end SHE offers *not* looking as the only solution: "It's your nerves. Close your eyes." When HE tries to spy on the neighbor from afar, he sees "nothing"—upon further reflection, he is sure that whatever he thinks he saw was just a "flaw in the window glass."

II

The poems in this volume were not included in any of Zbigniew Herbert's Polish poetry collections; although it is often impossible to establish on the basis of the archival versions why they were left out, it is fair to assume that reasons varied, from the poet's dissatisfaction with even apparently finished poems to political sensitivity and Herbert's habitual reticence about certain subjects like relationships and illnesses. Sometimes his feelings about a poem changed. The poem "Epic," printed in the first edition of his first collection, *Chord of Light* (1956), was subsequently removed. Slightly over half of the poems translated here were published in his lifetime, either in journals, anthologies, in translation, in editions of his plays, or in samizdat. Thirty-three out of these seventy-four poems were published only after Herbert's death in 1998, in magazines, editions of letters, and in the most complete "uncollected" collection to date, *Zbigniew Herbert: Uncollected Writings*. Its meticulous editor, the poet Ryszard Krynicki, gave the volume the subtitle "Reconnaissance" to emphasize the provisional nature of the enterprise and the hope of further discoveries and decipherings. Krynicki has transcribed many poems existing in Herbert's archive only in the form of handwritten drafts, often excruciatingly difficult to read.

In this selection from Herbert's voluminous *Nachlass* I have chosen to translate only poems existing in finished versions, even if, in some cases, it cannot be established which version is the last, or if there is a draft the poet himself considered final. Whereas Krynicki includes fragments and unfinished drafts, and provides justification for doing so—they are of value and interest to any serious reader of this poet—it seems to me that to present such texts with respect would require the kind of editorial apparatus and commentary that is not within the scope of this book. I included poems that were clearly marked or could reasonably be considered finished, those that can be read without extensive annotation and marked lacunae, and I focused on those that could shed new light on Herbert's work as a whole. The bibliography provides each poem's first publication and some basic biographical information where it is indispensable.

The emphasis in my selection of poems published posthumously is on poems addressed to friends, poems written in memory, and outings of Mr Cogito that add new facets to that persona. Among the aspects of Herbert brought into clearer view by the uncollected poems are his role as chronicler and elegist of his generation and his voice as a lover and erotic poet. In the 1950s, "Roll Call" recalls contemporaries fallen in wartime, and toward the end of his life, "Generation" elegizes the poets he considers his peers and allies across languages: Celan, Bachmann, Berryman, Plath, and others. They are his brothers- and sisters-in-arms in a different battle, the "cruel war called literature." The early lyric "So Much" connects love and the body's weight with the difficult rescue of speech or prayer, while in the later erotica of Mr Cogito, Herbert has adopted the rhetoric of silence, touch, and breath over the impulse to cast the poet or poetry as a saving grace.

If one thing emerges clearly from immersion in these writings, it is the line that runs from Herbert back to other poets of the fragility of human culture—to W. H. Auden, whose presence is felt along with Shakespeare's in "Epilogue to the Tempest"; to Osip Mandelstam, whose stark endgame in the Gulag is imagined as that of a desperate "court jester," a Joseph with a coat of many colors; and to Cavafy, who seems to flicker in the background of poems like "Contra Augustinum Pontificem in Terra Nubica Peccatorem in Purgatorio," where a bright presence from antiquity is briskly undressed, examined, and finally allowed to enjoy the grace of a generous historical skepticism. Because Herbert, too, conveys a tremendous joy in existence (as he says of Mandelstam), in earthly life and beauty, it is easy to lose sight of how stripped of all certainty, how courageous are his expeditions in "terror's deadly nightshirt," and how naked his encounters with what Auden calls the "artificial wilderness" shaped by human cruelty and blindness.

RECONSTRUCTION
OF THE POET

|:

PLAYS

THE PHILOSOPHERS' CAVE

Dramatis personae

Socrates • Guard • Council Emissary • Plato • Xenophon • Phaedo •
Phaedrus • Laches • Xanthippe • Crito • Keeper of Remains • Xantias

Chorus • Pupils

PROLOGUE

Music. Against a background din of drum and horns, the piercing voice of a piccolo. An empty stage, without decorations. The members of the chorus enter in short bright-colored dresses, pointed paper hats on their heads. Faces heavily powdered.

CHORUS I *with a deep bow*
A play about Socrates, son of a midwife and a mason.

CHORUS II
A tale with a hard pit.

CHORUS III
Full of words, allusions and pauses.

CHORUS IV
Unfortunately without action.

CHORUS V

Those who haven't brought food from home can still beat a retreat at this time.

CHORUS VI

Tickets will be refunded.

CHORUS I

A play, as has been said, about a philosopher.

CHORUS II

Who had a long life.

CHORUS III

Was active in the field of education.

CHORUS IV

But did not die a natural death.

CHORUS V

Which gives the figure a whiff of the sensational.

CHORUS VI

As well as a dash of heroism.

CHORUS I

One must exercise an inquiring mind through three acts.

CHORUS II

In order to untie the knot.

CHORUS III

Of lofty lies and shallow hypotheses.

CHORUS IV

Therefore we will have to avail ourselves of others' eyes.

CHORUS V

So there will be something here for the myopic and for the farsighted.

CHORUS VI

Least for those who see well.

CHORUS I

The author ordered us to apologize and to say that he will provide no answers.

CHORUS II

He says that he himself doesn't know.

CHORUS III

He states that if he knew, he would have written a work in German.

CHORUS IV

He wouldn't have summoned actors and tugged them by strings.

CHORUS V

There it is, though: he doesn't know.

CHORUS VI

And we, who have brought to its apex the art of agreeing to everything, will have to agree to this, too.

CHORUS I

A mitigating circumstance is the fact that the play derives from ancient times.

CHORUS II

A time when interrogation techniques were in their infancy.

CHORUS III

It was Socrates who came along and invented dialectics.

CHORUS IV

A practical manual for prosecutors wasn't developed until much later.

CHORUS V

Which is why the accused could work his mischief for so long.

CHORUS VI

And his head, washed up on the steep bank of our times, has had its features erased.

CHORUS I

We won't play a trick like that on posterity.

CHORUS II

All those exiled to the other world will have tied around their neck a tablet bearing the law they died for.

CHORUS III

All other materials will be destroyed, so that they don't constitute a temptation for psychologists.

CHORUS IV

A few of the innocent and infallible will be embalmed. We will also embalm their works and display them to the rabble. Entirely free of charge.

CHORUS V

In this way, humanity will be liberated from drama and from art, which is born of doubt.

CHORUS VI

And only history, demonstrated by geometrical proofs, will remain.

A sound like the lash of a whip.

CHORUS I

Let us begin.

ACT I

SCENE I

A stone prison building. Darkness. On a cot, a man covered with a cloak. Stairs on the left. A small window. ENTER Council Emissary and Guard.

EMISSARY

He's asleep?

GUARD

He's asleep. Sleeping is all he does. Noon and night.

EMISSARY

Is he ill?

GUARD

No. He says he's getting accustomed to death. Oh, he's an original.

EMISSARY

Wake him up.

GUARD

He asked me yesterday to leave him in peace. People are constantly coming here and tormenting him. Are you a pupil of his?

EMISSARY

No. I'm on official business.

GUARD

Ah well, that's different. *(He shakes the sleeping man's arm and yells.)* Man! From the murky domain of dreams, return to the barren and stony earth! I summon you!

> *The man on the cot wakes up, lowers his feet to the floor, rubs his eyes with his hands. The Guard laughs.*

EMISSARY

I've come to see you, Socrates.

SOCRATES

Aaaaaaah.

EMISSARY

Did I interrupt a dream?

SOCRATES

Yes.

EMISSARY

What were you dreaming?

SOCRATES

Nothingness—a gentle, soothing element.

EMISSARY

I get it, a bit like the sea. Do you recognize me?

SOCRATES

No.

EMISSARY

I'm an emissary, from the Council. I'm here on a mission.

He gestures at the Guard to leave them alone.

SCENE 2

EMISSARY

The day after tomorrow, as you know, the ship from Delos will arrive. That means that the day after tomorrow you will drink poison. You probably understand we dug up that old religious regulation to make it easier for you to escape.

SOCRATES

Yes.

EMISSARY

So the Council is disturbed by your delay. What do you think you're doing?

SOCRATES

I simply like the place. Before this, I walked the streets and my lectures had an accidental character. They were really just a collection of aphorisms of greater or lesser entertainment value. Now I have a school, like any self-respecting sophist. Thanks to you I'll be able to create something worthy of admiration: a system.

EMISSARY

Don't joke around. There's a rumor going around town about your last lecture, on the subject of the law. They say it was excellent, if quite reactionary.

SOCRATES

Well, well.

EMISSARY

In it you posit the thesis that laws should be obeyed.

SOCRATES

Yes.

EMISSARY

Even when they are cruel to us.

SOCRATES

Even then.

EMISSARY

I am an ordinary public servant, Socrates, and I would like to understand this properly. Because it seems a weighty matter.

SOCRATES

It is, no doubt about it.

EMISSARY

Just don't interrupt me when I'm speaking. Say: yes or no. Phoenician merchants say that in the African interior there are tribes who practice human sacrifice. That is their law. Lacedaemonian law decrees that weak infants be put to death. What do you say to that, Socrates?

Socrates is silent.

Of course you may say that our law has the people's wisdom behind it, and those other laws have the madness of tyrants. But when it comes down to it, isn't it all the same who wrote the law, one idiot or five hundred? What matters is that everyone agrees to it. Isn't it as I say?

Socrates is silent.

And how do we know they agree, how can we tell? Is it by the satisfied look on their faces, or by the processions of youths with torches? You know yourself only too well that this can always be arranged. So how do we tell? By the fact that everyone obeys the law, even if they rebel inwardly. So that your defense of the law, Socrates, is basically a defense of power. And absolute power at that. You're a totalist.

SOCRATES

Go on.

EMISSARY

For several years not a single death sentence has been carried out in Athens. The condemned walk out of prison in full daylight, go to Piraeus, board a ship and then write abusive letters from Crete or Miletus. Sometimes they send a few obols "for an unforgettable stay in the charming hotel at the foot of the Acropolis."

We know what pains you most. Not the lack of the philosophical culture of Athenian shoemakers and butchers, but the softness of Hellas. The youth repeat your aphorism: "Nothing strengthens the spirit and the flesh so much as early rising and the alternative."

SOCRATES

Is that all you've got to say?

EMISSARY

No, one more conclusion. You failed to cure us with logic, so now you wish to save us with a crime. You want us to smell your blood. You want a new power, even if it's that of tyranny and cruelty. Because only after that, you seem to think, can a new freedom and Pericles come, with symmetry, good architecture and poetry. And also the whole dignity of life, at present only accessible in the theater. At heart you're a politician with leanings toward a coup d'état. Why don't you say anything?

SOCRATES

I'm thinking of something with regret.

EMISSARY

What?

SOCRATES

That I have little time left and I've let loose a monster.

EMISSARY

Try to get it back under control.

SOCRATES

It's too late.

EMISSARY

It's never too late. You're still alive. I'll be back tomorrow. I'd prefer to find your cell empty.

SCENE 3

GUARD

I didn't like that new acquaintance of yours. A pupil?

SOCRATES

No. An official.

GUARD

That means he'll be broke, too. It's time, Socrates, to entertain some rich people. Isn't there some banker you know?

SOCRATES

No.

GUARD

Too bad. Because you see, in the first days the tax on your release is very low.

Then the cost of living is added to it. I'm not talking about myself. I have a fixed price: five obols. The crime makes no difference either. It's all the same to me, whether "drunk and disorderly" or "matricide." But first you have to come to an arrangement with those on top. And those on top say that there has to be a gradation. Otherwise we would be reduced to total anarchy.

SOCRATES
This hierarchy of values everywhere.

GUARD
Seems that way. For you, I have to say, I feel sorry.

SOCRATES
Why?

GUARD
That you don't have friends. So many people buzzing around you, but no one willing to spend a dime.

SOCRATES
There might even be someone who would. But you see, I'm old. It's a risk.

GUARD
Don't say things like that to me. If you had someone close, they would pay out for you. And you could escape. But like this—you'll perish. Do you have anything you could sell?

SOCRATES
Nothing.

GUARD

Right. I've seen your wife and kids—they look poor. You don't look like much either. At least get them to bring you a better cloak the day after tomorrow. I'd lend you one, but I'd be scared you'd run away to the other shore with it. *(Laughs.)* I'm really quite fond of you. But people don't like you. They say you're a know-it-all and you don't recognize the gods.

SOCRATES

Who says that?

GUARD

People.

SOCRATES

And what do you say?

GUARD

I don't know you very well. But I think people should be respected even if they believe in the gods. Religion is a beautiful thing. It's easy to love a wife who's sleeping right next to you, but Aphrodite . . .

SOCRATES

Do you believe in the gods?

GUARD

When it thunders, I believe. But I pray even when the weather's fine.

SOCRATES

Who to?

GUARD

To the heavens. My heart rises up and right away a warm glow fills my breast.

Plato appears on the steps.

PLATO

We're here, master. May I call them in?

SOCRATES

Come in. *(To the Guard.)* We are being interrupted. You can't even imagine how these lessons bore me. With you it's different. You go straight to the most important questions.

GUARD

Listen, Socrates. Talk to them. Maybe one of them will spend some cash on you. They say Plato has a lot of money.

SOCRATES

Okay, okay. Now go.

SCENE 4

ENTER pupils.

PUPILS

Greetings, master!

SOCRATES

Good day. Perhaps Xenophon will remind us what we discussed last time.

XENOPHON

Last time we pondered the truth of the equation: reason = good = happiness. We offered definitions of those concepts. An array of examples from life. Then we had a discussion.

SOCRATES

Who spoke?

XANTIAS

I did.

SOCRATES

We're listening, Xantias.

XANTIAS

A very wise man lived with us at Thebes, named Sophron. When his daughter died—he hanged himself.

PHAEDRUS

That's right. And no one said: "Sophron went gaga before he died," only "She was his only daughter."

PLATO

I asked you, Socrates, why Oedipus, who was undoubtedly wise and good, was not happy. Wisdom is one of the conditions of happiness, but then there's also fate.

PHAEDO

When I wake up at night and suddenly realize I exist, I feel pain. Then I repeat your catechism. "Who are you? A human being. What is a human being? An animal that laughs and reasons. What does a human being need?

To know. And happiness? Happiness is the child of knowledge." Then instead of fear I feel a void inside myself. I touch my face. Fear returns.

SOCRATES

I thought you had grown up to the level of abstraction, but I see you really only understand images. Well, what to do, there's not enough time to teach wisdom, so perhaps a few remarks from the sphere of hygiene. Laches! Apparently you are not a failed poet.

LACHES

No, Socrates. I studied sculpture.

SOCRATES

So you have the qualifications to be a philosopher. Imagine, Laches, that you are to sculpt Apollo's head in sandstone. What do you need to do this?

LACHES

Tools and a block of stone.

SOCRATES

Can you imagine a block of sandstone?

LACHES

Before you even said that, I had imagined it.

SOCRATES

You see, we understand each other very well. Then it will be a white cube. Let us suppose that it will be a cube with smooth walls and the ratio of width to length will prompt a feeling of satisfaction.

Now you strike with a hammer . . .

LACHES

Before I strike it, I think that the stone is going to perish, and I don't know if that which emerges from it will be more perfect than the simple cube with its beautiful proportions.

SOCRATES

Yes, but now you know that all things of this world are born of simple forms and one day return to them. Look coldly at the lines defining objects: you'll see triangles, circles, cubes. They are without color. They lie in space, as if laid there by a hand seeking order. Among all the senses the wisest are the eyes. The eyes protect the soul from confusion. You will be healed by the peace sent you by the line of a branch against the background of a winter sky. You, Phaedo, if you wake up at night, light a light. Don't lie in the dark, because then nebulous music will drown you. Light a light and observe the objects in your room. It doesn't matter what: it can be a sandal or the edge of a table. Learn the outer shell of the world before you set out to look for its heart. That's all for today. Now leave me.

They leave. It grows dark.

SCENE 5

SOCRATES *speaks to the advancing darkness*
When after the final question
a silence ensues
when the white pebble of calm
begins to crumble in my fingers
I hear—
through a silence as soft as fur
I see—

through black and white bands
of undulating air
two flutes
two horns
sticking out over the edge
of reality

You come Dionysus
murdered a hundred times
a hundred times risen from the dead
you who thrashed like a fish
in the net of syllogisms
you who were fatally wounded
by my mechanical
monster of dialectics
you whom I dragged by the hair
through the streets of Athens
you come and you say:
"I and my centaurs
will pronounce over your remains—worthy Socrates—
a solemn litany
of laughter"

And further:
"Miserable worm
you slaved away
wishing to liberate humanity
from disquiet from suffering from incarnations
so you grabbed the two words farthest apart
and stitched them into the silly formula
reason equals happiness

Do you hear the cackling
do you see how
Mother Nature's
most sacred belly
is shaking?"
And here is my answer:
Truly it is a misfortune
to be a blasphemer and do battle with the devil
and be vanquished by the devil in the end
for in all likelihood
the victory belongs to you
Dionysus
Perhaps reason—as you claim—
is an instinct unto death
an echo of nothingness
You have chased me into this cave
and surrounded me with a throng of characters
all carrying my name
that is your last temptation
O Tempter
They come and ask
Who is the true Socrates?
You want me to suffer vertigo
at the sight of my likenesses
and to save myself from madness
by falling to my knees before divine frivolity
and the sacred play of appearances
You have two nights Dionysus
to seduce me
I have two days
to learn endurance

and perhaps in the end
tearing off mask after mask
I will read my own face
with dying fingers.

Curtain.

FIRST CHORAL INTERMEDIUM

The stage as for the prologue. Three members of the chorus sit on the earth playing at dice.

CHORUS I
What news from town?

CHORUS II
Nothing.

CHORUS III
Price of onions is up.

Silence. The rattling of dice.

CHORUS I
They say there's going to be a war.

CHORUS II
Who says?

CHORUS I

Bankers.

CHORUS III

Well, they're always saying that.

CHORUS I

But the Spartans keep carrying out maneuvers on the border. There will be war, autumn at the latest.

CHORUS III

There will or there won't.

Silence. The rattling of dice.

CHORUS I

Slowdown at the port.

CHORUS II

The Phoenicians were supposed to come for earthenware and textiles.

CHORUS III

They didn't come. One thing is sure: the day after tomorrow the ship from Delos will arrive.

CHORUS I

About that—what's going on with Socrates?

CHORUS II

Still in jail. Everybody's telling him to run away. But he's dug his heels in. His daimon advises against it.

CHORUS III

Weirdo.

Silence. The rattling of dice.

CHORUS I

I'll tell you why Socrates doesn't run away.

CHORUS III

Well?

CHORUS I

He hates the sea. The sight of it alone makes him sick.

CHORUS II

Another proof that he's not a Greek. He doesn't like the sea, doesn't like boys. Doesn't like wine either. He's a freak.

CHORUS III

They say his maternal great-grandfather was a Thracian slave.

CHORUS I

Could well have been.

Silence. The rattling of dice.

CHORUS I

Who won?

CHORUS IV

Me.

CHORUS I

Are you going to go on playing?

CHORUS IV

We'll play to the end. And then once again.

ACT II

SCENE I

Morning of the next day. The same setting.

EMISSARY

Asleep?

GUARD

Asleep. He sleeps all the time. Last night he shouted in his sleep.

EMISSARY

What did he shout?

GUARD

I don't know. He called someone, then he chased them away.

EMISSARY

You didn't hear a name?

GUARD

No.

EMISSARY

Listen, do you people treat him well here?

GUARD

Of course we do. What do you think? He was just shouting like that by himself.

EMISSARY

How's the food in here?

GUARD

Not great. He says he's hungry. Sometimes he even drinks the oil from the cressets.

EMISSARY

Wake him up.

GUARD

Socrates! The gentleman from the Council. Get up. Enough sleeping already.

Socrates stirs. He rubs his face.

SOCRATES

Good day. Don't you realize you can't build a drama on such monotony?

EMISSARY

I've come for the last time.

SOCRATES

Well, so, begin.

EMISSARY

I'll begin. I stood over you for a long while when you were sleeping. Your face in sleep becomes like an animal's. Sunken temples, drooping lips, deep furrows down the middle of your cheeks—they all say the same thing: you're at the end of your strength. You sleep a lot, but sleep brings you no repose. You wake full of distaste and confusion. You feel your body escaping from you. Your arms and legs hurt; your heart can't keep up with your breath. There's only a name left to keep the separate parts together. And you long for the moment when another's hands will carve your name in stone. You're mortally weary, Socrates, and you're dreaming of a rest deeper than sleep. If that's not the truth, please contradict me.

Socrates says nothing.

That's normal. But what's not normal in you is the lure of theatricality. We know very well how you worked out in detail all your "accidental" meetings with your pupils in the street, in the woods or in the mar-ketplace. Foreigners liked all that, but we see it as a farce being put on. So now, feeling that death is near, you've reached for the tragic mask. Socrates who caught a cold returning from a banquet and died of pneu-monia, or Socrates dying in prison, condemned by the people who can't bear the weight of his wisdom? No doubt about what to choose. So you chose the easier way. Right?

Socrates is silent.

And about that school of yours. In a year or two it would fall apart for good. Young boys who come to you from far and wide don't want to study logic without end. They want to know how many gods there are, what the earth rests on and what happens to a man after death. Of these three questions you will have the answer to only one, and even that not until tomorrow. So you flee from loneliness and abandonment into death. That's your heroic act. Do you know what a commander does after a defeat?

SOCRATES

I do.

EMISSARY

There you go. Everything's been taken care of at the top. You can choose the method you prefer. If you like we'll bring you a medic who will painlessly open your veins.

SOCRATES

Thank you. In everything you say, I see only a great annoyance.

EMISSARY

What annoys me is the way you have got us tangled up in your death. We really didn't want to condemn you. Now we can't withdraw. So we appeal to your loyalty. By tomorrow you can vanish. If escaping *with* your body seems too hard to you—leave it here.

EXIT Emissary.

SCENE 2

GUARD

Well?

SOCRATES

Nothing.

GUARD

You're not well.

SOCRATES

You think?

GUARD

Everything's prepared up there. They say that if you want to, you can do it today. Everything's ready.

SOCRATES

You know, my friend, Socrates too has to be prepared.

GUARD

Eh, it's all the same to you—you're tough. They told me to encourage you. Tomorrow it's going to be swarming with people in here, women will come, there will be wailing. Today you can do it quietly, without a fuss.

SOCRATES

Yesterday you encouraged me to escape and again today you're urging me to escape.

GUARD

No, not today, not anymore. Now everything has been prepared.

SOCRATES

Not everything, not yet. Oh, even if it's just my pupils. I've caught my cloak on a bush and now I'm afraid to move—it would be such a pity about the cloak.

GUARD

I can see you're just telling yourself that, about the cloak. Fine, fine. If they don't bring it to you from home tomorrow, I'll lend you mine. You can't drink poison in a hole like this.

EXIT Guard.

SCENE 3

Plato appears at the top of the stairs.

PLATO
Greetings, master.

SOCRATES
How are you?

PLATO
We've just come from a chorus rehearsal. We're singing a fragment of Euripides at your funeral:
    O proud fruit of fathers,
    O fruit of proud mothers.
Tomorrow, everything as we decided?

SOCRATES
Yes.

PLATO
We'll come before sunset.
The last rays
fall on the head of the wise man
the pupils

with cloaks over their heads
step by step
go into
the night.

SOCRATES
Have you written an elegy?

PLATO
You don't understand. Whatever I touch I must name.

SOCRATES
Study geometry, Plato.

PLATO
It may come to that in the end. I'm not happy in the company of words.

SOCRATES
I'm aware of that.

PLATO
I see the world as if in a broken mirror—fragmented and in tatters. There's no connection between an object and its appearance, between the essence and the thought. I'd love to know even the smallest thing precisely from every side, from the center, from what it feels and what it is in the eyes of a star. If I knew that about the poorest stone—I would build knowledge of human and divine affairs.

SOCRATES
You suffer from appearances.

PLATO

Yes. The world is made up of appearances. Shadows everywhere, nothing but shadows. But where is the thing that casts the shadow?

SOCRATES

I've talked about this, Plato.

PLATO

You kept talking about man, how he should be, what courage is, what the good is. That's not what's most important. The most important thing is the world. The mysteries of cliffs, air, light and water. One must look at man as if at a thing. That helps to bear love and death more easily.

SOCRATES

A peculiar case. Two monsters fight over you: the monster of poetry and the monster of reality.

PLATO

I'll tell you something else. Recently a friend of mine died. The news of his death gave me a feeling of inspiration. I wrote a poem. Only later was I seized by true sorrow. I began to suffer.

SOCRATES

Write poems, Plato. The world must be fortified with false tears.

PLATO

Is that all you're leaving me with?

SOCRATES

That's all.

PLATO
Just a bit of mockery.

SOCRATES
More than that, Plato. A bit of irony.

SCENE 4

ENTER pupils.

PUPILS
Greetings, master!

SOCRATES
Welcome. What did we discuss at our last lecture?

PUPIL I
The usual thing, that reason equals happiness. And a digression about ways of looking. About perceiving the sharp edges of things.

SOCRATES
You'll have to forgive me. Today's lecture will be a little unsystematic. Because I am under the impression of a dream. I dreamed that I woke up at the bottom of a rocky ravine. It was night. Silence. Suddenly I heard a beat coming closer. It grew. Someone was rushing up to kill me. All at once everything went quiet, as if it had moved away. Silence. And again that horrible noise coming nearer.

PUPIL II
It's Dionysus visiting you at night, Socrates.

PUPIL III

He likes to come at night.

PUPIL IV

In our village he possessed three girls. They went into the mountains. Now they live with wild goats.

SOCRATES

Dionysus is gone. Two centuries ago he was ambushed in a rocky desert and flayed of his skin. You offer sacrifices to a decaying god. What I'm talking about is a question of blood. We have in us light blood and dark blood. The light blood washes our bodies and strengthens them. It defines the shape of a man. It gathers under the skull. The dark blood pulses deep in the breast. It is the source of the murky images of soothsayers and poets. If you hear a beat in yourself, that is the voice of the dark source. When it reaches the heart, there is no escape from terror.

PUPIL I

It seems to me, Socrates, that the dark source pulses not only in us. It is in the heart of all things: in the shivering night air, at the bottom of shimmering waters, and even in the yellow fist of the sun. For you the world is cut from stone. But you know, the heart of a stone sometimes trembles like the hearts of small animals.

PUPIL II

Terror is linked to terror; everything that lives and passes takes solace in terror. We particles of warm air, we flowers, we people unite against an irrevocable catastrophe.

SOCRATES

Even if it's as you say, our business is to fight our way through to what endures like a star above the chaos of sources.

PUPIL II

But may we betray the earth?

SOCRATES

There is no you, no shadow of trees and birds, earth and sky. There's only unmoving unity.

PUPIL II

Just a cipher.

SOCRATES

Without beginning, without end, unmoving, indivisible.

PUPIL II

Body and soul meet in the depths. In the dark interior of the earth they expire and give birth to new beings. Thousands of new creatures unlike anything that existed before, different from what will be later.

SOCRATES

Oh well. I can't persuade you. You're too young. Deafened by the quarrel of life and death. But one day you will leave that house full of noises. And there will begin your journey upward. To the unmoving, white, indivisible number. It's late now, go home.

SCENE 5

Socrates alone.

SOCRATES

I. Onward to You. An entreaty for You not to abandon me. That I may feel to the last Your cool hand on my brow. And Your unmoving eyes in my eyes. And Your radiance.

II. Give me a little more strength. You know how I love form and definition. I was always attached to the body and sure only of the body. So when they start to take everything away from me, from power over my legs to the last thought—please let me not cry out.

III. I don't know if You wish to salvage anything. They say that from the scattered bones You extract a flame that wanders the dewy meadows of the world. I don't want an immortality like that. If I am to go on existing in any form, make me a being that loves definition.

IV. Thank You for a life that passed so that I never renounced sobriety. I also felt no shame for the vertigo that comes from full consciousness.

V. I didn't praise Your name. I didn't bring sacrifices to You. I didn't encourage my pupils to practice Your cult, knowing that to You it is a matter of complete indifference. I praised you in conjunction and disjunction, and also in a little temple built out of syllogisms.

VI. So in the end I turn to You with the entreaty for You not to abandon me. Let me feel Your cool hand on my brow. And Your unmoving eyes in my eyes. And brightness.

He goes to the window.

Socrates greets the tree outside the window. Now we both know that everything that will happen, comes to us. One shouldn't look for fate, You said. You have to mature, grow upward, cast your seeds and shadows—and wait. Until what is to come, comes—accept it. Whatever it is: a spring breeze or an axe. I have a full head of gray hair and order. You have a full head of green noise. But it is from You that I learned the wisdom of endurance. Socrates bows down to Your roots.

Curtain.

SECOND CHORAL INTERMEDIUM

Three chorus members playing as before.

CHORUS I
What's new?

CHORUS II
Nothing.

CHORUS III
They say it's beginning.

CHORUS I
What?

CHORUS III
They don't say that.

CHORUS II

Stuff and nonsense.

Silence, the rattling of dice.

CHORUS I

I heard in town that Sparta's heading for a revolution.

CHORUS II

If they spill each other's blood, maybe there won't be a war.

CHORUS III

There will always be wars.

CHORUS I

Until the people take power into their own hands.

CHORUS III

Then . . .

CHORUS II

Yes, yes. Always the same thing.

Silence, rattling of dice.

CHORUS I

Speaking of. What's up with Socrates?

CHORUS II

In jail. Execution tomorrow.

CHORUS III

It's all pretty mysterious.

CHORUS II

I see political machinations there. Someone paid him gold to compromise our justice system.

CHORUS I

For me the business is simpler. Socrates makes the Athenians uncomfortable; no one really knows what's in him. They want to smash him open and see what's inside him.

Silence, rattling of dice.

CHORUS I

Who won?

CHORUS IV

Me.

CHORUS I

Will you play on?

CHORUS IV

We'll play to the end. And then once again.

ACT III

SCENE I

GUARD
How are you, Socrates?

SOCRATES
Good day.

GUARD
Good enough for me, but you, poor fellow, you won't see the stars tonight. I wouldn't want to be in your skin.

SOCRATES
It's not so terrible, only these last hours are dragging.

GUARD
See, you should have done it yesterday as I advised you.

SOCRATES
Listen, have you ever seen any executions?

GUARD
I've seen a few.

SOCRATES
Do you know what it feels like?

GUARD

With hemlock, it's pins and needles all over your body first. Then a numbing of the legs, as if you'd drunk strong wine. The head goes on working the longest. You can speak, too. Finally hiccups and tremors come. Well, and that's it. What comes after that you should know yourself.

SOCRATES

Oh, well . . .

GUARD

To make the poison act more quickly you have to walk around after drinking it.

SOCRATES

Oh, see, that's valuable advice. A real friend's advice.

GUARD

It acts faster on the young than the old. It all depends on how the blood circulates. So you have to move around. Today you have the right to a longer walk in the courtyard.

SOCRATES

I'll be glad to take advantage of that.

GUARD

Well, let's go then!

SCENE 2

Empty stage. After a moment Xanthippe enters. She sits on the cot. Sometime after her, Plato enters.

PLATO

Greetings!

XANTHIPPE

Greetings.

PLATO

You're waiting for him?

XANTHIPPE

I am. I thought it would all be over.

PLATO

We're waiting for the ship.

XANTHIPPE

Is it certain it will come today?

PLATO

Yes, it should already be here.

XANTHIPPE

It should be here. I'm worried. Yesterday he put his head on my chest and his shoulder started shaking strangely.

PLATO

Are you afraid for him?

XANTHIPPE

No, I'm afraid for myself. I'm old. There's no room in me for any feeling anymore. I want him to leave me just as he was—unknown.

PLATO

I wonder what it was that brought you together!

XANTHIPPE

I met him in the street, and then he started following me everywhere like a shadow. I felt his eyes on my hair, on my face, on my skin. Like Argus.

PLATO

Some would call that love at first sight.

XANTHIPPE

It was fear. At that time Socrates was a wiry young boy. He was liked—which is to say, average. The eyes looking at him were friendly eyes, they didn't expect anything.

PLATO

You mean to say that he found a question in your eyes.

XANTHIPPE

No, fright. I was frightened of him like I'd be of a wild animal. And I think Socrates concluded from that that there was an unknown force in him, and he started to look for that force.

PLATO

Socrates' force is his wisdom.

XANTHIPPE

You're wrong. Socrates' force was his mystery. He saw it in my eyes. Man himself is blind. He has to have mirrors or other eyes around him. He loves—that means he examines himself.

PLATO

And you discovered his mystery?

XANTHIPPE

No, Plato. You don't discover a mystery. It was Socrates' mistake, he took to it like untying sandals. Anyway, for me the most important thing was to free myself from fear. I thought the best way to do it would be to marry him.

PLATO

Forgive me but that's not very logical.

XANTHIPPE

Yes, it was a mistake. I remember that first night. He was heavy as a stone and silent. He wanted to hear the first word from me. If I had said: "Socrates, you will be king," he would have become king.

PLATO

And you said he would be a philosopher.

XANTHIPPE

No, I didn't say anything. I felt a painful embarrassment, so I shut my eyes and clenched my hands. He should have asked, like all men: "Darling, are you happy?" I would have lied to him and said yes, and from then on I would have been happy. I might even have loved him.

PLATO

But hatred came instead.

XANTHIPPE

Well, you see, very simple things can be reasoned out. Yes, it was hatred. It followed him like an enormous shadow. And again Socrates thought that he was great. For the second time his greatness locked itself in me, in my hatred.

PLATO

One might think that there was no Socrates outside you.

XANTHIPPE

But there was. When he saw that he wouldn't get anything out of me, he ceased to notice me. When he spoke to me, he avoided my name, he was even scared to use demonstrative pronouns. He would say: "Mother should concern herself with raising children." Or: "Mess in the kitchen shows disorder in the soul." Not being able to speak directly, he began to think abstractly.

PLATO

That's really going too far. You overestimate your influence, Xanthippe. The true Socrates, what I will call the public Socrates, is a creation of his pupils. When they discovered him a dozen or so years ago, he was like a street singer, clearly a talent, but without any culture. He didn't know Homer, his dialectics were amateurish, and he had no metaphysical interests—in a word, a primitive. A whole system of finishing his education was worked out, by presenting him with supposedly random interlocutors, from a shoemaker to a sophist. A tremendous labor.

XANTHIPPE

We're arguing over the true Socrates as if we were playing dice for his coat. We can agree on a provisional definition: the true Socrates is the one who must die.

PLATO

Yes, he must die because of his philosophical school. He shone bright in the intellectual firmament of Athens and he must be extinguished, before people start analyzing the brightness, before they ask Socrates for a system. Only we know that there is no system. To preserve that secret, we must sacrifice Socrates. The rest belongs to commentators.

XANTHIPPE

Socrates must die so that Xanthippe does not fall in love with him. When he leaned his head on my chest a few days ago, I felt a wave of tenderness I'd never known. He was small and helpless. What do you think, does he fear death?

PLATO

Ah no, why would he. After he solved the problem of the immortality of the soul.

XANTHIPPE

I'm not asking what Socrates thinks of the soul, I'm asking if he fears death.

PLATO

You can ask him yourself in a minute.

XANTHIPPE

Do you think he'll be sincere?

PLATO

Sincerity is the last mask of the living. The next one, death puts on.

XANTHIPPE

And what is that one called?

PLATO

Peace.

SCENE 3

ENTER Socrates.

SOCRATES

Welcome! You've come to say farewell?

XANTHIPPE

Yes.

SOCRATES

Well, so—farewell, Xanthippe.

XANTHIPPE

Farewell, Socrates. I don't feel sorry for you.

SOCRATES

Thank you.

XANTHIPPE

Everything that made us different from each other seems unimportant now. Is there nothing else you need?

SOCRATES

Many things, Xanthippe. But I have to try to get them for myself.

XANTHIPPE

What should I say to our sons?

SOCRATES

That their father was thinking of them on his last day and asked the gods to make them grow up to be honest citizens. What do you think, Plato, will they resent me for dying in prison?

PLATO

No fear of that.

SOCRATES

I don't think so either. There's no fact about which all Athenians think alike. So farewell, Xanthippe, thank you for everything.

EXIT Xanthippe.

And now you, Plato. What should I wish you?

PLATO

I have a last request for you, Socrates.

SOCRATES

What?

PLATO

May we be present at your death?

SOCRATES

Is that necessary?

PLATO

You promised.

SOCRATES

Well, yes, but I still have a lot of things to discuss with myself.

PLATO

We won't bother you while you do that. We'll come right before the execution. You'll be like a hero dying with a chorus in the background.

SOCRATES

Well, all right, all right. Though I'd prefer that chorus to be someone else.

PLATO

And will you tell us something about the immortality of the soul? I feel that would be the most appropriate conclusion.

SOCRATES

Go now, Plato. Don't come until right before the execution.

Socrates moves into a corner. Now a reflector casts an enormous shadow of a spider's web, in which he is trapped like a fly.

I called for you a long time today; you must have been busy. You were probably observing. I confess that's the role I most like you in. Two vigilant corals of eyes and that perfectly controlled compassion. People say there's also a certain mark of sadism. I don't know. I only know that sharp observation is half of philosophy. The other half is a strong net. It's important that it be unnoticeable in the first moment. The victim feels caught by the wind. He believes he is battling the elements and so relents. Only later does he see the thin threads wound around his body. Then you can begin to prove to him, with the aid of arguments based on rational assumptions, that he will die. I did it all completely differently. I supposed that my victims were reasonable animals, so I started from definitions, syllogisms, and only later, very discreetly, did I show them the perspectives of metaphysics. You turned out to be the better psychologist: first paralyze them, cast them into the abyss, and then give them an exegesis of fear, suffering and other such things. Well, so you have a better method. Given the unprovability of the conclusions, this means you have the better philosophy. In any case you had the easier task. Your victims were generally weaker than you. Whereas between me and the specimens I hunted there was no difference in genus. My net had to be strong, it had to prompt confidence. When I got caught in it myself, I couldn't show them I could tear it off like a spider's web and step onto the other side of freedom. It's a question, you understand, of respect for one's own net. A moral riddle.

SCENE 4

Crito is led in by the Guard.

CRITO
You called for me, Socrates.

SOCRATES
Oh Crito! Please sit down. I'm in great need of you.

CRITO
Must be some kind of testament.

SOCRATES
Nothing like that. I'm preoccupied here with the silliest things. Do you re-member the name of that friend of ours—a little guy with red hair? He lived near us on the corner of Sandalwood Street. We played together.

CRITO

You must mean Menaikhmos. Later he moved with his parents to Miletus. Harelip.

SOCRATES

That's the one.

CRITO

Menaikhmos . . . red hair . . . with a harelip . . . Very strong. He beat everyone at arm wrestling. But at wrestling you were better. Once you had someone in a double grip—no chance . . .

Both laugh.

SOCRATES

And do you remember our boat races?

CRITO

Of course. The best boats were made of bark. They never sank. To make them sail faster you put a piece of lead in the bottom. The season began in the north bay in mid-April. The finish was near the little bridge. The winner took his opponents' boats. Once you beat Menaikhmos. He couldn't handle losing; he lay in wait for you and hit you with a rock. He opened up your forehead. We thought he'd killed you.

SOCRATES

When I got home my face was covered in blood. But even so, my mother gave me a hiding. And all the boats went into the stove. Yes, yes, Crito, every victory is laced with defeat.

They laugh.

CRITO

Yes, yes, Socrates. At school they didn't know what to do with you. Later when some mischief was done and no one knew who had done it, they said: "It must have been that devil Socrates."

SOCRATES

And that whole lark with the May bugs, remember that?

CRITO

And when you set a fire in the hall? You almost burned the whole building down. Antiphon squealed as if he was being flayed of his skin.

SOCRATES

Antiphon was the grammarian?

CRITO

No, the one who taught geometry. Unbelievable bore. He talked through his nose: "Pay attention, numbskulls! What is equal to the tangent of alpha? The tangent of alpha is equal to . . ."

SOCRATES

Was he the one who didn't like finding grass snakes in his pockets?

CRITO

He was. You know, sometimes I dream I'm taking an exam. They ask and I can't say anything. I don't even know the sum of the corners in a triangle.

SOCRATES

Oh, those were ancient times.

CRITO

Golden times, despite us having our hands and rear ends red from punishment.

SOCRATES

How many of us are left?

CRITO

In Athens only two. The rest emigrated or croaked.

SOCRATES

Why are you looking at me like that?

CRITO

I'm searching your face for . . .

SOCRATES

For what?

CRITO

The scar from Menaikhmos' rock.

SOCRATES

It must have healed. That was a long time ago.

CRITO

Come closer, it was just over the arch of your eyebrow. There it is. Small as an obol, but it's there. Yup, no doubt about it.

SOCRATES

Thank you, old man. To have a man around who remembers our childhood at a time like this—it really helps.

CRITO

I'll shut your eyes. Can I do anything else?

SOCRATES

No, we've had our chat.

CRITO

I just think these memories make a man soft.

SOCRATES

Not a bit. Now I can say with complete serenity: "There once was a man called Socrates."

SCENE 5

ENTER pupils.

PLATO

Socrates, the ship has come in.

SOCRATES

That's good news.

PUPIL I

We came to say farewell.

SOCRATES

Farewell to you. Don't hold it against me that I didn't teach you very much. Teaching is a difficult business. You'll find out when you become fathers.

Pupils stand in an expectant attitude.

I see you are waiting for a farewell speech. Something about the immortality of the soul, Plato said. But maybe better to talk about the weather? About light frost at night and the vines might freeze? But the shepherds say soon a warm rain will fall and green will cover everything. Green will cover everything.

CRITO

Listen, dears. Don't torment him now. We will be here with him till the end, we'll close his eyes, say a prayer and go home. But now let us give him some peace.

All are silent for a long moment.

SOCRATES

They're coming!

CRITO

No, you imagined it.

SOCRATES

I'd prefer to speak now.

An hour before my death my friend comes. About that: I said "my" death. That pronoun is very typical. What does it show? It shows that we try to assimilate the phenomenon, adapt it in a way. That seems to us the only right thing to do. The other option: to take it as a violence and rebel. That leads to religion or to madness. A philosopher ought to assimilate necessity. But now the set time doesn't seem right to me. It is an abstraction, and an abstraction wrongly constructed. It contains a long stretch of time called dying. All that emptying of the eyes, heavy breathing, propping oneself on an elbow, the heart failing, then a moan with the last breath, and finally that stiff strangeness and the body's stubborn silence. Those different states are described with one word. Such a short word, like a knife cut.

Now I want to direct your attention to the continuity and the many phases of the phenomenon. It is a stunning thing that you cannot find a point from where the process begins, or a point when it can be considered definitely over. This leads to the conclusion that life is full of death, and death full of the spasms of life. In other words, we die from the moment we're born, and you in the bloom of youth are dead up to your knees.

Calling geometry to our aid, we can imagine it as a vector or segment AB, along which point X moves. It gets more complicated if we want to imagine it as a circle. After running the whole track, X finds itself back at the point of departure. That would mean the possibility of traveling the whole road again, which taken to its logical consequence leads to the notion of infinity and immortality. This is a more interesting concept, no doubt, because the first one—unconnected segments that suddenly break off—leads to chaos, even if we set over it a mechanical necessity or another concept uniting those shreds in a rational image of the world. Which one to favor . . . but I think this time they're coming.

PLATO
Yes, they're coming.

ENTER two guards and a boy holding a chalice. Socrates drinks. He walks back and forth. After a moment he stands still. He sways. The pupils grab him under the arms and support him to his cot.

GUARD
Your legs have already gone, poor man.

SOCRATES

After a moment, slowly, each word separately.

Don't forget to offer a rooster to Asclepius.

After a moment, feverishly and incoherently:

Yes, Polos . . . justice . . . sacrifice . . . whole life . . . Apollo. Polos . . . remember . . . whole life . . . why . . . there's no.

Silence.

PLATO

Before we take a mask, let us record his last words: "Don't forget to offer a rooster to Asclepius." What came after that was gibberish. Let's write down the last words so there won't be any disputes later.

PUPIL I

How do you understand it?

PUPIL II

It was just some sacrifice owed that he suddenly remembered.

PUPIL III

Eh, that would be banal.

PUPIL IV

And he was never sick anyway.

PLATO

I understand it as a figurative statement, something like a great metaphor.

PUPIL III

A great metaphor?

PLATO

Yes.

Curtain.

EPILOGUE

CHORUS I

What's new?

CHORUS II

The whine of mosquitoes.

CHORUS III

It's a real plague by now.

CHORUS IV

Little Furies.

CHORUS V

Everything is little these days.

CHORUS VI

The gods and their epidemics, too.

CHORUS I

And apart from that, silence.

CHORUS II

Silence and malaria.

CHORUS III

Malaria marks the boundary of civilization, and silence, pangs of conscience.

CHORUS IV

People aren't silent now about anyone but him.

CHORUS V

Who?

CHORUS IV

Socrates.

CHORUS I

Yes, that was a bad business.

CHORUS II

Innocent blood was spilled.

CHORUS III

It will have to be redeemed.

CHORUS IV

He was burned at the state's expense.

CHORUS V

Some people are bickering about a monument.

CHORUS VI

Maybe even a beatification.

CHORUS I

Oh, here's the Keeper of Remains.

CHORUS II

He always has something sensible to say.

CHORUS

And fresh news.

KEEPER OF REMAINS

Good day, what are you discussing, dear citizens?

CHORUS IV

Socrates.

KEEPER OF REMAINS

In a sublime and mystical tone or a bloody patriotic tone?

CHORUS V

More the former.

KEEPER OF REMAINS

Nonsense, my dears. The case is simple. Socrates came from the proletariat. His father made his living in a workshop, but he himself couldn't do that anymore. Competition, big workshops, manufacturing, you understand. He had to go out on the street and earn his keep by jabbering—economic conditions turned him into a philosopher.

CHORUS IV

And who turned him into a martyr?

KEEPER OF REMAINS

He did—or more precisely: his misunderstanding of the mechanism of history. As a prole he should have expressed the strivings of the proletariat. He would have become a people's tribune, an agitator. He had the program ready: the struggle with the reactionary upper middle class, seeking contact with its progressive lower depths. It's so obvious. But he preferred the aristocracy and its favorite disputes: about what is good and what is evil, about abstract justice, from the moon. Well, and he fell from the moon straight into prison. That's how you pay for being a traitor to your class. Well, farewell. Exterminate mosquitoes and idealism.

EXIT.

CHORUS I

You know what? Let's play dice.

CHORUS II

Good idea.

CHORUS III

We'll play.

CHORUS

We'll play to the end and then once again.

RECONSTRUCTION OF THE POET

Voices
Professor • Homer • Elpenor • Woman's Voice

The PROFESSOR *always begins the same way, like a recording switched on in the middle.*
. . . eece. Fragments have been excavated . . . in part of the lower . . . of Artemis in Miletus.

Discovered at the beginning of the twentieth century by Evans, it has not been fully studied. Evans was led astray by a thick layer of matter, hardened like rock, under which he didn't think anything would be found. We have taken into account a source which is admittedly quite late, from the period of the Persian Wars, I'm thinking of Apollodoros of Dioros, and Euthyphro the Elder, a second-rate historian, but quite reliable, who . . .

Water drips from the tap.

. . . expectations and constitutes a watershed event for scholarship. In the part we call the Third City we have discovered the oldest known inscriptions of the Homerides, which constitute without any doubt fragments of the *Iliad* at least two centuries before the final official edition of the epic as it was passed on to our times. The expedition to Milos, working parallel to us, has also discovered written sources, which however are without artistic merit (I will mention them in parentheses at the end), important only as a confirmation of our thesis that there was a lively center of artistic endeavor in Asia Minor, and not on the peninsula, which . . .

Water drips from the tap.

. . . who was this Anonymous? We only know this: that he was Greek, but from the fragments he left we can reconstruct his portrait.

So above all, he was a man at the height of his career and happy (valuable remarks on the goldsmith's art), a forceful personality, striking to all for his tremendous calm and self-control. No nervousness, a complete absence of the exaggeration in the use of the means of expression, which is sadly such a grievous flaw in contemporary art. And above all—one would like to cry out—no raising of the voice, harmony in emotions, harmony in speech. He looks even upon the cruelty of war with the cold eye of the true epic poet. Noble measure and dignified gravity clothe these shards in simple and sublime robes. A profound knowledge of life permits him to touch on a wide variety of themes, which can be divided into seven groups:

1) themes of war
2) themes of mythology and genealogy
3) themes of love
4) pastoral themes (a valuable passage on grazing sheep)
5) themes related to metallurgy (bronze, copper, iron)
6) themes of daily life
7) other

Water drips from the tap.

. . . and the following fragment, for example, testifies to Anonymous' power
of poetic imagination:

Soft-footed Hermes hurries to the bedside of Gorgias,
who supports the canvas awning of the tent with his snoring,
and Hermes whispers into the ear of the sleeping man
that he must take the side of Gymed, whose father
held Lemnos, rich in wheat; and his older brother,
mighty-fisted Atarchos sailing through the Hellespont
chased Apollo's rage for Briseis, taken by force,
of whom Castor was born, the cause of evil, too brash,
he abandoned his father, white-bearded Nikos . . .

A crash of breaking glass.

HOMER *shouts*
Enough! I can't listen to this parody. First Virgil, then the translators, phi-
lologists, archaeologists . . . There's nothing left of me but a handbook of
mythology and a model for teaching stylistic analysis.

I am forty-five years old. I live in Miletus. Wife, son, a house with a garden.

I like Miletus a lot. It's a lively town. Just the right amount of noise you need
in order to live. A healthy climate. A keen and well-heeled public.

To begin with I worked on a ship. But I had an accident. I fell on the deck
and lost my eyesight, the doctors said it was shock, that it would pass. But
it hasn't worked out very well. I was no longer suited to work at sea, so I
worked in the port as a foreman. I always had a good voice. Strong as a gale.
My friends persuaded me to give a recital. I did—and it caught on. I would
be really happy if it weren't for these eyes. Doctors tell me to spend as much

time as possible in the dark and to stay out of the sun. My wife locks me in the house. I have to find ways to escape. It's a bit ridiculous. I can't stop now, just when I'm at the peak of my success. In a few years I'll be able to retire. I'll buy a big hotel in the center of town. Full of life and noise—from the cellars, where they roll barrels, to the whisper of lovers in the cheapest attic rooms. Then I'll spare my eyes. I'll squint at the world that comes to me. I'd also like to work on the theory of epic. I think I've accomplished a little bit in that field.

For my predecessors the epic was a vast plain. They pounded the drums for battles, processions, razed cities and fires, in a monotonous voice. Everything seen from far away and therefore very shallow. I went into the fray. I made the epic a mountain, heavy matter that lifts itself up from the earth to the heavens and reaches all the way to the gods.

My predecessors mastered emotion by mastering their voices. A silly ploy and a slander against nature. I discovered the human need for the cry. As long as terror lives in man, we need to cry out.

Now it's noon. The city is white with heat. Everything is covered by quiet dust, but underneath there's a cry.

WOMAN'S VOICE
Where are you off to, Homer?

HOMER
I'm going for a walk.

WOMAN'S VOICE
But you know . . .

HOMER

I know, I know.

WOMAN'S VOICE

You know they were hurting yesterday.

HOMER

But better today.

WOMAN'S VOICE

Don't go into the market square. Promise.

HOMER

I promise.

WOMAN'S VOICE

And avoid the sun. Elpenor, watch your father.

ELPENOR

We're being disobedient again.

HOMER

Tough luck, my son. I can't stand sitting at home.

ELPENOR

Why?

HOMER

When it gets to be noon, the silence is unbearable. You can hear the wasps buzzing in the attic. It makes my skin crawl.

ELPENOR

You have peace and quiet. You can compose poetry.

HOMER

I don't think of poetry at those times.

ELPENOR

What then?

HOMER

Nothing beautiful, my son. Flatbread with onions smells better than marble. And I'd give an Ionian head for a head of cabbage.

ELPENOR

What's attractive about that?

HOMER

Everything, silly boy. The color, the smell, the noise. All the voices of life: the muttering of beggars, the squeals of girls pinched in the crowd, the guardsman's drum, the cries of the produce merchants and the baying of the animals tied by their horns. Then the poet comes and a battle begins.

ELPENOR

A battle?

HOMER

Yes. I have to outcry them, stifle them, take their voice away, swallow it and then bring it back out of myself.

ELPENOR

That's real suffering.

HOMER

And joy. At those times I'm as full up as the world.

ELPENOR

That's what I don't like most, when toward the end . . . your voice rises and you start shouting.

HOMER

Why?

ELPENOR

It's as if you were scared and crying for help. Are you scared at that point?

HOMER

No. I'm doing battle.

ELPENOR

With whom?

HOMER

With terror.

Voices of the market.

Well, here we are. Let's get to work.

ELPENOR

Citizens! The poet Homer, renowned on the mainland and on the islands, has decided to give a recital, ceding to your pleas, and despite the pressure of work. For the first time you will hear a description of the seventh battle at Troy. A work completed at dawn today and as yet unpublished. A portion

of the revenue will be dedicated to religious purposes: the purchase of glass
eyes for the statue of Hera.

HOMER *against a background of rising music*
Dawn. Rosy rain falls on the sky's tin sheet.
A first rustle in the bay. A bird smothered in its sleep.
Rising from marshes, pale mists, quiet as the dead.
Already in the tents of animal hide ruffled by wind
you hear the sound of metal crashing on metal and voices
carry the day, full day, day unwound from night
like an infant from its swaddling clothes, drinking glorious air.
First Agamemnon inspects the ranks, spurs them on,
Piramides is with Archimedes, Castor, Eurylochus and Pandar.
Hooves, the rattle of clubs, cries, the creaking of carts
awaken the Trojans, so that the gates open with a clattering;
two battalions, infantry and cavalry, tight as a fist,
stand in the milky darkness, bright as a distant wood.
Agamemnon takes his sword. He cools it in the open air
then warms it with a grand gesture, knocks it against the sun
till you hear the groan of iron—and at that a stifled cry.
They set off. The noise is mighty, like a giant's sandal crashing down on
stones, stone against stone, metal on metal
and leather strap, the magnificent din of the material world,
but people are still mute, caught up in the rush and the thought
of the dead waters of Erebus—
Eurylochus is right by Ajax, who urges him (remembering
the dream and the prophecy, the broken column of smoke)
"Take care, friend, to steer clear of the Trojan archer."
A javelin rips the conversation apart. Ajax's coachman
falls, his cry is short, like broken reins tugged
by maddened horses. Terror common to beasts and men,

hair stands up under the helmet, sweat and shaking knees.
So in order to conquer fear, the Greeks raise overhead
the vast shield of a cry. The battle is fierce and beautiful.
A roar as pleasant to the gods as the fat flesh of sacrifice
rises high and in the heights reaches divine ears
rosy from sleep and bliss, so the gods descend to earth.
Thus the epic begins. For what is an epic but a thick knot
of men, iron and gods, locked together in convulsions
with a red rooster on top. That rooster praises terror, that . . .

A sudden pause.

HOMER

Elpenor!

ELPENOR

I'm here with you, Father.

HOMER

Let's go home.

ELPENOR

What happened, Father?

HOMER

Guide me home.

ELPENOR

But you have to finish. Everybody is waiting.

HOMER

Home.

They walk away from the noise. A pause.

Slow down, my boy. Something's happened to my eyes.

ELPENOR

Are they hurting?

HOMER

No.

Pause.

Come here, son, and look me in the eyes. What do you see?

ELPENOR

Myself in the middle. And trees. And the city.

HOMER

But I don't see that. Nothing. Nothing.

ELPENOR

You only see darkness? Like before, when this happened to you.

HOMER

I don't even see darkness. Nothing.

Pause.

ELPENOR

You're tired, Father. The stones give off a white glare.

HOMER

White, you say.

ELPENOR

Yes. Is that strange?

HOMER

No, that's normal. The strange thing is what I have in my eyes at the moment. It's not even blackness. It's the color of the void.

> *Pause.*

I have no idea what's happened. What do you think?

ELPENOR

You'll go home and get some rest.

HOMER

But I can't have gone blind.

> *Pause.*

When I sang of the death of the coachman, I was still seeing very well. I noticed Sefar left a slaughtered ram, wiped his bloody hand on his coat and moved toward us. At that moment I had them all in the palm of my hand. I was happy.

ELPENOR

You know what, Father—why don't you close your eyes. I'll guide you. If your eyes are shut you'll get more of a rest.

HOMER

Yes, you're right. It's calming.

ELPENOR

There you go.

HOMER

It's ridiculous to have your eyes open and see nothing.

Pause.

Do you think when I open my eyes I'll be able to see?

ELPENOR

Of course you will. But don't do it right now. There's no rush.

HOMER

Right. There's no rush.

ELPENOR

Maybe you'd like to sit down?

HOMER

I would, but first let's get out of the city. The walls are closing in on me like water.

Pause.

ELPENOR

You sang beautifully.

HOMER

That was from fear. I felt fear from the moment I got up today. I wanted to kill it with a cry.

ELPENOR

You killed it with poetry.

HOMER

Poetry is a cry. Do you know what's left of an epic when you cut out the clamor?

ELPENOR

I don't know.

HOMER

Nothing.

Pause.

What do you think? Tell me it won't stay like this.

ELPENOR

I'm sure it will pass. Don't you feel any better?

HOMER

Better, yes. But for the moment I'd rather not open my eyes.

ELPENOR

Sure.

HOMER

Let's sit here. Where are we?

ELPENOR

By the fountain of Pan.

HOMER

Well of course, I can hear it. It's only a few steps from home.

ELPENOR

We aren't in any sort of rush.

HOMER

You're right, my son. Let's not hurry.

Pause.

When I have my eyes closed, I calm down. But I'll have to open them in
the end.

ELPENOR

Let's give it a try when we're back at the house.

HOMER

All right.

ELPENOR

What are you doing, Father?

HOMER

I'm checking my face. Everything present and correct. My eyes are where they should be. A horrible feeling, when something so much your own suddenly abandons you.

ELPENOR

It's nice here.

HOMER

Yes, it is. Peaceful, shady.

ELPENOR

Lie down on the bench. I'll cover your face with my cloak.

HOMER

You take care of me like Antigone took care of Oedipus. Only Oedipus really was blind. Say something, son.

ELPENOR

When we buy a hotel, you won't have to leave the house. The sun bothers you.

HOMER

Yes. It really bothers me.

ELPENOR

The hotel will be among trees. In the shade.

HOMER

We'll have to call it something.

ELPENOR

"Under the Snoring Merchant." That will attract merchants and thieves.

HOMER

Or "Under the Eye of Zeus." That will attract pilgrims and moderate atheists.

ELPENOR

We'll have a lot of servants.

HOMER

And good wine. Only the two of us will have a key to the cellar.

Pause.

ELPENOR

Father. Let's go.

HOMER

All right. We'll go. It's not far now, right?

ELPENOR

Just around the corner.

HOMER

I know it by the gravel: now I see with my feet.

ELPENOR

Well, and here's the house now. Our house, Father. Look.

Homer cries out.

PROFESSOR

. . . eece. As I have remarked, the second discovery has no real significance. Anonymous of Milo in comparison with Anonymous of Miletus is a dwarf next to a giant.

Water drips from the tap.

. . . unimportant and commonplace themes. Anonymous does not hesitate to dedicate a poem to the tamarisk, a vulgar, invasive plant without any use.

HOMER

I told of battles
towers and ships
slaughtered heroes
and heroes who slaughter
and I forgot that one thing

I told of a storm at sea
of walls collapsing
grain set on fire
and hills plowed up
and I forgot the tamarisk

when he lies
pierced by a spear
and the mouth of his wound
closes up
he doesn't see
either the sea
or the city
or a friend

he sees
a tamarisk
right by his face
he climbs
onto the highest
dry branch of the tamarisk
and passing
the brown leaves and the green
he attempts
to fly off into the sky
without wings
without blood
without thought
without—

PROFESSOR

The insignificance of the theme goes hand in hand with the atrophy of form, which . . .

Water drips from the tap.

HOMER

Well, what can I say, I'll admit it. I wrote about a tamarisk. How did it come to this?

On the third day after the incident at the market I left Miletus. Alone. A sort of pilgrimage to a sacred place. The sacred place was the island Milos. The spring and temple of Zeus the Miracle Worker.

There was an enormous crowd at the spring. In accordance with the instructions of the priests, one had to sprinkle oneself with holy water and state one's request out loud. The roar was indescribable. "Hippias asks for his amputated leg to grow back." "Antyclea begs to be able to give birth again and for her husband to come back to her." I shouted loudest, in a voice dark and thick with tears: "Homer demands his sight be restored!" Three days, and no miracle.

At night I went to the temple and repeated my request. My voice wound around the columns, hit the ceiling and fell flat at my feet. I clung to the altar and touched the god's face. His lips were shut tight as mussels. He was as blind as I was.

I took pity on him, and to console him, I composed a little ode.

For a long time I cast upward
the coarse rope of my cry
to drag you down to earth
the noose came back empty

now I know
neither from blood
nor from bone
nor even
from the body of thought

only in a great silence
can you sense
the pulse of your existence
unceasing and piercing
like a wave of light

attractive
like everything that doesn't exist

I pay tribute to you
touching the body
of your absence

I didn't have much time to concern myself with the god. More important
things were going on. My body was ripening in the dark and the silence. It
was like the earth in spring, full of unanticipated possibilities. My skin grew
a new sense of touch. I began to discover, explore and describe myself.

First I will describe myself
starting from my head
or better from my foot
more precisely my left foot
or from my hand
from the little finger of my left hand

my little finger
is warm
slightly bent in the middle
ending in a nail
it is composed of three segments
it grows straight from my palm
if it were separate
it would make a sizable worm

it is a peculiar finger
the only little finger of the left hand in the world
given directly to me

other little fingers of the left hand
are a cold abstraction

with mine
I share a date of birth
date of death
and a common loneliness

only the blood
chanting its dark tautologies
binds together distant shores
with a thread of mutual understanding

I began to study the world very carefully. Everything I had known about it until then was useless. Like a set from a different play. I had to learn anew, starting not with Troy, not with Achilles, but from a sandal, from a buckle on a sandal, from a pebble struck carelessly in the road.

the pebble
is a perfect creature

equal to itself
mindful of its limits

filled exactly
with a stony meaning

with a scent that doesn't remind you of anything
doesn't scare off anything doesn't arouse desire

its ardor and coldness
are right and full of dignity

I feel a heavy remorse
when I hold it in my hand
and its noble body
is imbued with false warmth

pebbles cannot be tamed
to the end they will look at us
with a calm and very bright eye

I'll never return to Miletus. My cry stayed behind there. It could sneak up
on me in some alleyway and kill me.

Between the cry of birth
and the cry of death
observe your fingernails
the sunset
the tail of a fish
but what you see
don't carry it to market
don't sell it at bargain prices
don't shout

the gods like lovers
like a tremendous silence
between the roar of the beginning
and the roar of the end
be like an untouched lyre
which doesn't have a voice
it has all voices

This is only the beginning. A beginning is always ridiculous. I sit on the lowest step of the temple of Zeus the Miracle Worker and I praise my little finger, the tamarisk, pebbles.

I have neither pupils nor an audience. Everyone is still fixated on the great fire of the epic. But it is already dying out. Soon there will be only blackened ruins, which the grass will vanquish. I am the grass.

Sometimes I think that maybe I will manage to lead new people out from new poems, people who will no longer add iron to iron, cry to cry, terror to terror.

After all, you can add a grain to a grain, a leaf to a leaf, an emotion to an emotion.

And a word to silence.

PROFESSOR
. . . eece. The impoverishment of the poetic world of Anonymous of Milos supports the assumption that he had no successors and that . . .

THE OTHER ROOM

Dramatis personae
He • She • What's on the Other Side of the Wall

1

SHE
I can't look at her.

HE
Turn away.

SHE
I did.

HE
Today?

SHE
Yes. She comes into the kitchen. "Can I boil some water?" She takes off the pot. She puts on the kettle. "Chilly today." I don't say anything. "What have you got against me?" I turned to the window. She takes the kettle and goes out. Now we'll have some peace.

HE

You think?

SHE

She has big ideas. Just don't go talking to her. Not a word. Crickets.

HE

How will that help? She's not going to move out.

SHE

But we'll have some peace.

HE

You're right. She'll stop telling the story about her daughter who got too hot at a party, drank some water and died.

SHE

You've been spared. Me, she's told about everything: giving birth, weddings, her aunt's romances, her uncles' advances. What sort of mushrooms they liked and how they looked in their coffins.

HE

She's alone.

SHE

So what?

HE

At the beginning she said she'd be like a mother to us.

SHE

Thanks but no thanks. Plain egotism. Why wouldn't she go into a care home?

HE

Old people fear a home like peasants fear a hospital. It's where you go to die.

SHE

Got to somewhere.

HE

Better at home. People are ashamed of death. They know they'll be lying there askew with their mouths open and you will be able to do what you like with them. Better at home.

SHE

It's all the same.

HE

You've got to have something of your own. A sheet, a pillow.

SHE

In life. But after?

HE

After, too. A patch of earth, a wooden cross.

SHE

Why? To mark a spot that relatives visit.

HE

Not that. You want to have something. It protects you. When a person is naked, he dies. She is protecting herself, too: with three pots, a screen, a door key.

SHE

Death comes in by the chimney.

HE

And finds us at the table with a mouth full of bread.

Pause.

SHE

There's no point getting sentimental. We have to manage. Why did we worm our way in here?

HE

Who could have known this would go on for three years? It seemed like it could happen any minute.

SHE

I knew.

HE

You know everything, but you don't say anything.

SHE

And did you ask?

HE

Let's stop.

SHE

That's right, let's stop.

HE

What do you want?

SHE

For you to find a solution.

HE

Want me to whack her with an axe?

SHE

Don't shout. You're not scary. You're ridiculous.

HE

I've had enough of this.

SHE

It was your idea.

HE

So?

SHE

Now I'm the one having a hard time. You're away half the day.

HE

Talk to the old lady. Tell her we're expecting a child.

SHE

She'll be over the moon. She loves children.

HE

Offer her something extra. Old people like money.

SHE

I'm not going to talk to her.

HE

Well, then we'll rot in here.

SHE

Can she live long?

HE

Could be long. She doesn't do anything.

SHE

But she eats poorly. Milk, porridge.

HE

Enough for her.

SHE

How old is she actually?

HE

Seventy or eighty.

SHE

If she's seventy she'll live another ten years.

HE

You can't predict anything. She could always get sick.

SHE

A cheering thought.

HE

Right, we're powerless. We can only wait.

SHE

Let's send her a letter.

HE

What kind of letter?

SHE

Make it look official. "On the grounds of the decree of such and such a date you are ordered to vacate an illegally occupied property." An illegible signature. And send it off by mail.

HE

We could try it. We've got nothing to lose.

2

HE

Did she get it yet?

SHE

Yesterday at noon.

HE

Well, and?

SHE

Well, you can see. Nothing.

HE

It must have spooked her?

SHE

Probably.

HE

Won't she guess who wrote it?

SHE

I don't think so.

HE

And she won't check?

SHE

How can she? She never goes out.

HE

True. But it must have had an impact on her.

SHE

For sure. She's been locking her door from yesterday.

HE

That's not good either. She's withdrawn too much.

SHE

She could die and we wouldn't know.

HE

We should listen in. Quiet.

Pause.

SHE

You can't hear anything. She's probably in bed. She's been looking unwell lately. She didn't get dressed. In her bathrobe all day. Her skin was yellow and dry. She probably doesn't sweat or cry anymore. Dying is drying out.

HE

Even her eyes have dried up. Sometimes I was afraid they'd fall out like marbles.

SHE

She's lost a lot of hair lately. Before now she used to wear a little bun. Not long ago she was standing with her back to me. I saw that the middle of her head was bald. You could see her pink, freckled scalp.

HE

And she walks as if she were held together with string. If you tugged hard it would all fall apart.

SHE

We have to pay attention now. Keep listening all the time. Shh, quiet.

Pause.

HE

You can't hear anything.

SHE

She's too light. The floor doesn't creak underneath her. It's only in the morning and at noon you can hear she's cooking.

HE

When I was little, I caught a hedgehog. I put it in a shoebox and tied it up with string. I talked to it. I'd tap my finger and it would move. Then it stopped.

SHE

What are you getting at?

HE

Nothing. Just a memory.

3

SHE
Give me a break.

HE
Oh.

SHE
Stop it.

HE
Why?

SHE
I can't right now.

HE
You're all worked up again.

SHE
When we're alone.

HE
We are alone.

SHE
She . . .

HE
What about her?

SHE

She'll be getting up, going to the wall and listening.

HE

Nonsense.

SHE

Let's wait until she's asleep. In the summer we had that little room by the sea. Away, in the little loft. Only bats on the other side of the wall. We were happy.

HE

Fourteen days.

SHE

Soon we won't even be able to look at each other anymore. I know you by heart now. Sometimes I feel like leaving.

HE

You have to lose each other and then find each other again. That's what it takes in love.

SHE

We could go away together.

HE

Where?

SHE

To another city.

HE

In another city it would be the same.

SHE

It's the same everywhere.

HE

Sometimes I want to run and shout.

SHE

Shout what?

HE

Aaaaaaooooooooh! Like that.

SHE

It's so cramped it chokes me.

HE

There are too many people on earth.

SHE

They get on each other's nerves.

HE

In the end we'll be packed in tight from ocean to ocean. Old folk will be drowned off the coast.

SHE

Quiet. She's moving. Listen.

HE
I don't hear anything.

SHE
It was like a bed creaking.

HE
You imagined it.

SHE
Quiet. Now.

Pause.

Right. Nothing. It was yesterday evening when I heard her last. It was quite clear. Something fell on the floor.

HE
Maybe she fell.

SHE
No, it was a lid.

HE
And then nothing.

SHE
Nothing.

HE

It's been twenty hours.

SHE

What do you think, what's going on over there?

HE

I don't know.

SHE

I don't know either.

HE

It would be worth having a look.

SHE

You're crazy!

HE

I don't mean go in. But have a look.

SHE

I tried through the keyhole. Can't see anything. There's something white hanging on the door handle.

HE

Quiet. Something moved.

Pause.

SHE

It's the clock.

HE

If it's ticking, she must have wound it yesterday.

SHE

Not necessarily. Old clocks only have to be wound up once a week.

HE

You're right. But I'd like to know.

SHE

It'll become clear sooner or later.

HE

No reason to be alarmed.

SHE

The most important thing is for us to stay calm.

HE

You know, I have an idea.

SHE

Well?

HE

Let's test her. We'll pretend to be hanging a picture on the wall. It'll sound like we're knocking on her door. If she reacts, it'll be proof.

SHE

Good idea. But why hurry. We can do it tomorrow, if nothing has changed.

HE

Right. There's no rush. Rushing it may spoil everything.

4

HE

Well, how are things?

SHE

Nothing. Nothing this morning either.

HE

What do you make of it?

SHE

Something's happened.

HE

But what?

SHE

I don't know. Sometimes it's better not to know.

HE

For now. But it's got to be settled somehow. One way or the other.

SHE

Yesterday you said you'd knock.

HE

I can knock. Forty hours have passed by now.

He knocks, they listen.

Nothing.

SHE

No movement at all. Knock again.

He knocks, they listen.

Why did you knock more softly this time?

HE

I didn't knock more softly at all. I knocked the same, even a little harder.

SHE

No. You knocked softer.

HE

It doesn't matter. She's not answering. Maybe she's asleep?

SHE

If she's a heavy sleeper she won't wake up.

HE

All the same, I'd prefer to know.

SHE

Yesterday it was quiet, but today is quieter.

HE

I don't get it.

SHE

Yesterday it was quiet, but today is quieter.

HE

What does that mean?

SHE

Not quieter, but more muted. Yesterday it was as if there was someone there, but sitting quietly. Today it's as if no one's there.

HE

Do you think she went out?

SHE

I don't think that at all.

HE

Did you not smell anything in the hallway?

SHE

What was I supposed to smell?

HE

Well, some kind of smell.

SHE

I smelled nothing.

HE

Nothing? Maybe the smell of medicine? That would mean she's sick. If we could smell it, we'd know.

SHE

Yes. That would be information.

HE

Maybe I should knock again?

SHE

There's no point. Better to look.

HE

But how?

SHE

You can see her window from the building opposite.

HE

Well, and?

SHE

You can go into the stairway and look.

HE

You think I'll see anything?

SHE

You can try.

HE

Doesn't she have curtains on the windows?

SHE

No. She has white lace curtains halfway up the windows.

HE

That's good. It's evening, you can see inside.

SHE

Are you going?

HE

Yes.

SHE

I'll go with you.

HE

You don't have to.

SHE

My eyesight is good.

HE

But someone should stay here and listen.

SHE

But there's nothing to hear.

HE

Something could happen at any moment.

SHE

Will you come back soon?

HE

I'll have a look and come back.

5

SHE

Why were you so long?

HE

Were you afraid?

SHE

You said you'd be right back.

HE

I wanted to look at something.

SHE

Well, what?

HE

Not much.

SHE

Was it dark?

HE

No, but the stairway window is a little to one side. You can see the corner of a shelf. A chair in the middle of the room. Underwear hanging on the chair.

SHE

That means she's in bed.

HE

Probably.

SHE

Too bad you can't see the bed.

HE

I leaned out but I couldn't see it.

SHE

That would have moved the situation on.

HE

What do you mean, moved it on?

SHE

What else did you see?

HE

Nothing.

SHE

No movement?

HE

Once something flitted by. But it was just a flaw in the window glass.

SHE

That's all?

HE

That's it.

SHE

Not much.

HE

The important thing is that the light is on. It's very bright in there. The ceiling light and probably some bedside table light.

SHE

She never had the light on so long.

HE

Right. Unless she's alone. People feel lonely in the dark. Even the radio or TV can't console them. When we went out, she used to have all the lights on. She was afraid of the dark.

SHE

Why did you say "was afraid"? You think she's not afraid anymore?

HE

It doesn't mean anything. Did you hear anything?

SHE

It seemed to me that someone cried out. But that was probably on the street.

HE

Probably on the street.

SHE

It was a high-pitched cry. That's the way young people call each other. Anyway, maybe I misheard it.

HE

Most likely. Anyway, there's nothing going on there anymore.

SHE

You think this is the end?

HE

The end of what?

SHE

You said yourself there was nothing going on anymore.

HE

That means there's peace.

SHE

Quiet, rather. Another kind than yesterday even. Like an abyss.

HE

It's your nerves.

SHE

I'm sure.

HE

Peace is the main thing. We have peace. It's quiet.

SHE

Can we try one more thing?

HE

What?

SHE

Turn the radio on loud and open the hallway door. If she's asleep she ought to wake up.

HE

Let's try it.

SHE

Go into the hall and listen.

Loud music.

HE

Turn it off, damn it!

SHE

What happened?

HE

This is awful. It doesn't make any sense. Now we should have peace.

SHE

How long will it last?

HE

I don't know.

SHE

We have to make some kind of decision in the end.

HE

We're doing all we can do.

SHE

We should go in there.

HE

Let's leave it till a little later.

SHE

I think it's really about time.

HE

Let's wait till the morning. It's nighttime. Everything looks different in the morning.

6

HE

You're not sleeping?

SHE

No.

HE

Why?

SHE

I can't.

HE

I can't either.

SHE

I'm afraid to sleep because I might dream.

HE

I never dream of anything.

SHE

Better that way.

HE

Maybe better. When I fall asleep I feel as if I'm dying.

SHE

That's unpleasant.

HE

Nothing hurts. Something separates from us and then can't come back. It floats over the closed body and has no way of getting back in.

SHE

Let's talk about something more cheerful.

HE

What will we buy when we win the lottery?

SHE

A car.

HE

Or a little house. A car and a little house.

SHE

What brand of car will we get?

HE

We don't know what our coupon will be for. Well, and we don't know we'll win.

SHE

You don't know how to dream.

HE

Go to sleep if you can. It's late.

SHE

I can't. Let's talk. Where will we go in the summer?

HE

Where we always go. To the seaside.

SHE

Or maybe the mountains.

HE

When it rains in the mountains you feel like hanging yourself.

SHE

When it rains at the seaside you feel like hanging yourself, too.

HE

We could go to the mountains for two weeks and two weeks to the seaside.

SHE

Exactly.

HE

Only then all the train fares will add up.

SHE

But we're only talking about it.

HE

That's all right then.

SHE

What time is it?

HE

Dawn soon.

SHE

I don't like dawn. As if someone poured ether down your throat.

HE

Try to go to sleep.

SHE

I can't.

HE

It's as if we were holding a vigil for her all night.

SHE

Don't talk about her now.

HE

In a few hours it'll all be behind us.

SHE

We'll be free.

HE

I'm tired to death. I haven't done anything, but I'm tired to death.

SHE

It's your nerves. Close your eyes.

HE

I wish it were all over.

7

HE

What do you think, are we sure now?

SHE

I think so. The lights were on all night over there. They're on now, too. Who has the lights on in the daytime?

HE

Maybe she's just weak.

SHE

It's been too long.

HE

What do we do?

SHE

There's no use waiting. We have to go in.

HE

And if it's locked?

SHE

Doesn't matter, we have to go in.

HE

Maybe it'll take longer.

SHE

I can't wait any longer. Do you want me to go with you?

HE

Stay here.

SHE

Come right back.

HE

I'll have a look and come back.

Pause. He comes back.

It's over.

SHE

We have to open the window right away.

HE

And send for the doctor.

SHE

You look pale.

HE

I have to sit down for a minute.

SHE

How does she look?

HE

Good. It must have happened recently.

SHE

We should lay her out before she's too stiff.

HE

Maybe we can ask the caretaker?

SHE

Better to take care of it ourselves. We should behave like a family. Otherwise someone else will get their hands on the room.

HE

It's going to cost us a bit.

SHE

Tough.

HE

And a lot of errands to run.

SHE

Take a leave from work.

HE

We should send for a doctor. There has to be a witness statement. We can't wait too long.

SHE

You think they'll examine her. They'll just touch her and fill in a form.

HE

Whatever it is, we have to get it over with.

SHE

Best make the call.

HE

Yes, I'll just sit another moment.

SHE

Would you like some water?

HE

I haven't done anything, but I'm tired to death.

SHE

We should pack up her things and take them down to the basement. We'll just leave the bed. Till they take her away.

HE

We have to air out the room. It needs a lot of airing.

SHE

The floor should be waxed properly. Is there wallpaper in there?

HE

Yes.

SHE

We should tear it off. And paint.

HE

It should be a bright color.

SHE

Yellow.

HE

Yes, yellow. So it'll always be bright.

‖:

UNCOLLECTED
POEMS

GOLDEN MEAN

By night
they quaff pure air
devoid of dreams

Dreams are for Freud for those who tell fortunes
and for those who believe in the end of the world

       Scientists invent a beginning
       Prophets foretell an end
       We believe in a middle
       Snug as a drop of fat

       The mean has scent and color
       The bounty of three dimensions
       A million things made familiar—

They rap their knuckle on my disquiet
When I speak of the bottom and border
People in the middle people of the mean
blind as water

They don't believe in the end of the world
they'll tell you the earth is round

***FINGERS SPINDLES OF SOUND CAUSE OF MELODY

For Jerzy Zawieyski

Fingers spindles of sound cause of melody
Before you put them to strings to converse with the air
Put them to your own face may your breath wash them
Think how Jan Sebastian discovered heaven's key
which before he came opened nothing more than a stave

Fingers spindles of the line wise draftsmen
Apply them to white sheets of paper refined by form
And they defy the mutability of years free of anguish
Princesses painted by Holbein stitched up in smiles
whose lips are the scales of future constellations

Fingers spindles of verse lines O youthful poets
Weigh them long on your lips before touching a page
So we hear over the world's havoc the drowned colors
Flowers' scent of farewell and the transience of words
The voice the single voice that calls to us

PACIFIC I

Ex-soldiers
will feel pain
in amputated extremities
when they read newspapers
the same as before
       "Runner" wants to be a guard
       He quit the Unknown Soldier
             He'll swim down trenches
             a bullet will take his face
             He will return to the Unknown
             in a recumbent position
       Papers the same as before
       black with hatred
             POWs sleep in the noonday heat
             in the shade of acacias and papers
             and their faces are stung by abuse
             "just you wait—after the harvest . . ."
Combatants see the most clearly
they who have no right of speech
cannot raise their hands

Listen listen what they're saying:

The sun is hidden by a cloud
The sky is hidden by a banner
stitched from empty sleeves—

PACIFIC II

A little man
half a man
with the face
of a brazen beggar
hands to shove in the street
and to hold a peaked cap
on which you can play out
a parody of military honors
and add to that
the silly abdomen
of an insect
incapable of flight

This man
sways when he walks
like the tongue of a bell
like the heart of war
the heart of fury

TWO STANZAS

I. AUGUST

Womenfolk leaning on rakes like Pallases on spears
Grow huge in the shadows sent them from the sky's torn
overcast ceiling; fiddles silent as lutes
Beyond bridge and echo—laughter of distant metaphors

To those departing in shadows drawn out by the sunset
The harvesters bring a lost report of us
Who were startled at Pompeii—cut in silence like amber
We faint with the utmost hush in the assonance of dusk

II. SEA

When you rush up to me as noise and vision
And grow in my eyes as the simplest figurative wave
The string snaps like a shoreline and I don't know
If I'll conquer you with the oar of ancient measures

Odysseus found a twig from Ithaca
And bids the horizons farewell—dead landscapes
Finished epics. A commotion and constant noise
A poem flares on the breath—rose bouquet of winds

FRA ANGELICO: THE MARTYRDOM OF SAINTS COSMA AND DAMIAN

Left side of the painting

On the left the gestures of Pharisees
faces set falsely
a thousand doubts in the folds
but in the slits of the eyes a hard certainty

Priests of toppled altars
soldiers of a crooked oath
backs leaning against the city
look on the martyrdom calmly

Stark blue sky a gleam on helmets
and in their hands bows sharp spears
mutilate the left side of the heavens

      stone upon stone
      coarse comb of walls
      in the stone shooting ranges
      a burnt-out sky

      a tower lonely as a mast
      a tower deep as a stifled cry

they raise the heads of long-haired prophets
on deep tin dishes

This is the city
and its people of stone
this is the left side of the painting
and the world

Background

A hill—the earth is moved, the extended sigh of clouds
the sky open to blue, a journeyman's blue
and five willows, five elongated willows
five angels—
Too late.

Right side of the painting

You gave us words
tender hands

weeds for wounds
and agony

and the roar of angels

And now silence
the swish of a sword

And mortal sweat
and waiting

for a stone from David's catapult
Only winds cut off the wails
only a cut-off horizon trembles
Too great a scale—

Grass is better than people
it deepens the olive green
for a moment the head drowns
and then emerges pure
without the dew of human fear

DE PROFUNDIS

Caught in the net of taut veins
tightly upholstered in tough skin
pierced through by earth's axis

—I'm not a star

love cracks our knuckles
layers of suffering grow
a body bends and breaks

—I'm not a crystal

bound to people and to the world
rooted in the solid earth
subject to alien movements of planets

—I cannot be either remote
or perfect

    Subject to change
    near to death
    from a body's red pit
    —I cry out

SO MUCH

How hard
to save a person
who loves

I always feel
your slender arm
heavy as a body

It runs through my fingers
like water

Your breath
my pallor
and care

How hard
to save a person
who trusts

I bend over your sorrow
I lift the weight of love

I lift you from earth in my arms
carry you on my lips
give you up to prayer

CHURCH

In a cathedral's stony forest
under skull vault and sky
an hour of stopped clocks
the ashes of burnt grass

uncertain bonds of whispers
sighs for our daily bread
overhead mammoths' ribs
a sea and shore of stone

the silence of a pond on which
grows a sinful woman's hair
a season lonely as a kernel
breaks the bedrock and base

in the organ's birch forest
Sebastian lost a canticle
Jan found it and they went
embracing wing in wing

he was here too but was silent
he snuffed the altar like a sunset
the world left its footprints
in the lush meadow of the air

EPIC

1

I call with the voice
of a prophet inspired:

shut the door
shut the door
for the love of God

So badly do I fear
kitchen smells drafts
revolution and uninvited guests

I shut the door and windows
I shut them I shut them

And only a sparrow
hopping on the parapet
fills me with tenderness

I'm very sorry
that I'm not Saint Francis
and that barley is so expensive

I have nothing
dear little bird
Look
my pocket is torn
treasures drowned in my trouser legs

2

Although it's already late fall
the weather's glorious

A sky of uttermost blue
the sun is shining
without warming

That's why the delicate throat
is wound twice around
with a crimson scarf

That's why there's a felt hat
on the priceless head

So long
I'll be back for dinner

With the face on tribute money

3

At dusk Francis knocks

Please
sit Francis

He sits down
and lays his yellow fingers
on the tablecloth

Well there
—little by little

Minute by minute
in a circle around the clock face
our journey

REED

A little vapor
a drop of water
as Pascal says
will suffice

yet here we have
showers of comets
a stony cloak
and living fire

and here
ten bronze tablets
guarding
five cowering senses

give us death
up to our shoulders
up to our mouths
up to our brows
no higher

a little vapor
a drop of water
will suffice

ROLL CALL

So many times
so many times I have to say
Present
when they read the roll
of the living and the dead

it's a little schoolroom lie
and it's what I owe you

You come at night
wearing feathers from ripped eiderdowns
black angels of the ghetto

from a forest
smelling of pine needles and blood

from trains
as long as a death from starvation

in your hands
there is neither complaint nor iron
in ink-stained fingers
you bring echoing seashells a page from the atlas

a plan for an escape from the house
and a trip to the moon

this is a little mutiny of the imagination
and it's what I owe you

Then a great interval comes
memory's eyelid is lifted
during the interval we wage an attack
passing on our fingertips
a ball as light as victory
an unexploded shell

I must finish
your cutoff words
complete your smiles
welcome the air with my mouth
take in the hands lying alongside the body
a bitter grain of hope
the stolen fruit of love

it's a small labor of memory
and it's what I owe you

so many times
so many times I have to repeat
Present
when they read our roll
from which I won't let anything
be erased

COMPOSITION WITH BIRDS

they encircled the world with barbed wire
the heart beating behind the windowpane

but we my brothers will sing to them
to the colored braids the square ribbons

beyond the crumbs and the round eyes
and beyond the predatory alien fingers

we will keep for them in our trembling beaks
a drop of love until the end of the world

TO FLORA (ECLOGUE)

An earth fragrant with myrtle a heaven of plane-tree green
the heavy weight and sweetness of Flora's ripened eyes
A cicada praises the heat amid sweltering rocks
and brimming baskets of clouds cross the bay on the wind
a thick braid cascades down a neck of blood and milk
and startled by the setting sun comes undone on her shoulders
Don't hide your tresses Flora let them flow in watery streams
and don't turn your gaze away from the vineyard and the sea
as dark mountain water spills into the jugs of hushed valleys
nightingale replaces cicada evening descends in the leaves
We shall sing Flora's praise we will find wine and olives
Corydon will come with his syrinx and will play for us

LITANY TO IRONY

And what will be what will be
you ask in terror
if in the end love even love abandons us
this great warm powerlessness
forgiving gentleness
and the affirmation
that what is is good
that you must wrap yourself around the living
cast your hands' net over things over people
even the neck of the void

so if this abandons us
what will be what will be

enter Irony
patroness of the defeated

we hide our hands behind our backs

a petal of bitter wisdom
will fall on our lips

the eyes sunlit gardens of dreams
will castigate their colors
and we will behold in garish light
a huddled mass of creatures
convulsed by a shudder
of lust and hate

NIKIFOR

1

Baroque poets
on their title pages
commend themselves to the memory
of golden and purple lords

through corridors of syntax
up the steps of adjectives
they climb stairways
full of courtiers

Nikifor
contemporary painter
has no Maecenas

He opens his plain invocation
with the declarative sentence
that he is an orphan
and his occupation is painting

the next sentence
contains a little sophism

in its risky use
of the words *because—therefore*

because he is poor
and has nothing to live on
therefore you should buy
Nikifor's pictures

then with the same concern
he worries he has no underwear
or painting supplies
asks not to be abandoned

the whole thing ends
with a virile salutation
as if he were ashamed
of having said too much

2

In a battered tin box
live crumbs rainbows
colorful pebbles
from which the Lord
composed the mosaic of earth

a fragment of storm
a fragment of leaf
a fragment of water

with a threadbare brush
like a mouse's tail
one delicately touches
the pebbles of the world

before that
one has to animate the brush
which means moisten it

3

when the city appeared
true as if out of a dream
the master took from a church banner
three fat saints

he dressed them in black tailcoats
attached bow ties to their necks
gave one a top hat
and the other two bicycle helmets

he let them loose in a clear sky
like three heavenly carp
may they now sail
across the summer evening air

the sky is very luminous
so bright you can see clearly
big spiky letters
on the other side of the paper

it is a school exercise
on the theme of the Sad Life
of the Rural Proletariat
in Very Ancient Times

LOVERS

he sees how she
takes off the landscape
over her head

from the arm of the chair
a flowery meadow
slips carelessly

she comes on tiptoe
to take her place
in his arms
happiness seen is nothing
compared to that known by touch
look

they are good people
gentle descendants of conquerors
they wish for nothing more

they feed on their own breath
take up so little space
sleep like roots intertwined

in the triangle of the neck
breast and cheek
a soft warmth pulses

a little animal awoken
rubs against the heart
they close their eyes

indifferent that the tree they grew
so quickly sheds its blossom

white flowers of winter
green flowers of summer

ON THE REPATRIATION OF BRUNO JASIEŃSKI'S REMAINS

When the thaw reached
the Far North
the poet's body emerged
from under the ice cap

his grave so shallow
body only half buried
a daisy in one ear
a little grass in the other

but taken all in all
he was in very good shape
so they freshened him up
wiped the mold from his lips

blew on him and slapped him
doused him with jasmine
farewell dear poet
off to your fatherland

his fatherland is happy
the academy overjoyed

no one says: they killed him
they all say: he came back

they scream and shout
the crowd lifts him up
so you see my old pal
no need for living legs

at the author's evening
obedient comrades
whip him into shape
make blustery threats

and attached to his strings
the poet steps up to the mic
a little stiff but confident
he wants to read his poems

His hand in his wig
his voice makes the megaphone squeal
he grunts stamps and gestures
and they all say: he's so alive

the poem ends with a shriek
he raises a hand and screams
the string snaps and the arm
drops woodenly on the table

so as to erase the image
the cry goes up: long life

and presidium and poet
go off to have a drink

his wife is at the reception
but she behaves differently
when looking at her husband
she sobs into a handkerchief

champagne caviar oysters
pineapples and wine
poor man no more will you
drink water or feed on clay

but the poet eats nothing
doesn't even clink glasses
pale he goes off to one side
begins to wind his shroud

but no one notices this
alcohol flows like a stream
and it's only near dawn
they yell: he's gone and died again

NIGHT

Then, mirrors dissolve and there is nothing but the sound of dark water in
the mouth. This is happiness, so it doesn't last too long.

Soon we stand before an empty frame. They carry in two burning moths
across a creaking floor. Then on the cold glass, skin flayed from the face
appears, right between the smoking hair and the neck bursting into
flame.

ON THE NECESSITY
OF SCHOOLING

They learn to walk
with left
and right

they touch objects
frown
as if reading a difficult book
The Propaedeutics of Reality

they quit the microscope
come down from the tower
give man a good look

It's just that in midsummer
they still wear big fur hats
to cover their donkey's ears

(as in paradise
shame
signifies the beginning
of morality)

It's just that they still
aren't able to speak

from a tight throat
comes barking

barking about freedom
barking about the people

you have to begin at the beginning
instead of speeches
start a school notebook
to draw vertical strokes
circles lines

so as later
to build from it
the sentence
this is our house

MY STAR

My star is still growing in the earth. The soil is a bit moist. I'm worried that my star may rot before it ripens. I'd really like to move it up on a hillside where it's dry, but I'm afraid it will wither during the transfer. An astral sprout like this is very delicate. I think I step around it well.

To see a star you don't have to climb a tower. You have to take the earth on your face.

LITTLE LAMENT

I ask the day:

"Have you seen her?"

"No," says the day.

It takes a gigantic step toward me. It seems to wish to help. It pokes around with the end of a pointed stick, but all it digs out are old papers.

I ask the night:

"Have you ever touched her silent body?"

The night shrugs. It sits hunched over the sky's ashtray. Puffing at the stars.

It's the hour between brightness and darkness, narrow as the crack in the window frame where you may come upon dried spiders.

DECEASED

he never had anything
to hide

on top he wore
an open face

a defenseless
gentle neck

and hands
for grabbing flesh

when his old
father died
tears on his cheek—white mice

    so why now
    when he lives
    in a coal box
    in a narrow bed
    where the cold stream of his body
    flowing gathers
    the murk of candles

so why now
when he lies
with his face turned
to the gloomy ceiling
is he so wise and noble

he never had anything
to hide

on top he wore
naked skin

LITTLE TOWN

The little town
is bolted and locked
with the azure key
of lake and forest

Pens of the west
wrote a story
but chroniclers' pens
kept silent

only a photographer—
historian praises
fat babies
weddings and funerals

I could live here
as if on the bottom of a box
in an old wasp's nest
in a broken clock

—my little town this
little town
runs on its own

no one winds it up
from the froth of dawn
to the froth of death

GROVE

The grove is seasoned with boletus mushrooms. Sometimes a dried elf rustles in it. But the crowns celebrate the gold of sunset. Thus does sublimity grow from earthiness.

BOX

The walls converged into infinity. They gave off a hush of the zenith. A crumb of dust shone red in a crevice like a planet. Only a cloud sailing by with a stupefying odor of sulfur made me realize where we were. Our entire universe is shut up in a matchbox.

FUNERAL OF
A HIPPOPOTAMUS

He died in inconsolable grief. He was so oversensitive that a wasp flying by gave him palpitations. When he wallowed in mud he directed his gaze to the lofty azure. With azure in his eyes he closed his eyelids for good.

Now after death he grows ever thinner. You can already clearly see his delicate profile. Nothing will remain of him but a smudge of azure.

COLANTONIO — S. GIROLAMO E IL LEONE

To Karl Dedecius in enduring friendship

Truth be told it's a mess
all the books jumbled up
Organon Marx Engels Lolita Tractatus Logico-Philosophicus
the saint reads everything
and in the margins
a sprinkling of commentary:
compare page 7 quite right doesn't follow

on the desk scrolls of parchment
a pen an inkpot an hourglass
useless flasks that aid concentration
reflected a world upside down and thus cast into doubt

just as he was reading aloud
the prophecy of Saint John
a lion entered and held out
his paw pierced by a thorn
with a long Latin stylus the saint removes the thorn from the gray pad

this could have ended well
but it ended badly

the lion became very attached
followed the saint everywhere
trampling all the flowers
frightening the butchers
only undaunted children
yelled "stupid Leo"
and threw stones

the saint did what he could
he hid inside the gates
told his servant girl to say "the master is not at home"

—nothing whatsoever
the lion roared and swished its tail
driven quite mad
by love

on the day the saint died
the lion departed through filthy outskirts
straight into the desert

and it was then that it saw
the scarlet cardinal's hat
with the triple cord with fourteen knots
that the saint used to cover his aureole
when he went to the pharmacy on the corner
for headache pills
ascend slowly

like a moon
into the sky
all golden
now to remain there

forever

***THE MOUNTAINS FINALLY TURNED

the mountains finally turned
from shifting violet to black
this is their heraldic color
dignity's hue

only the insides worked
below the line of quiet

without any spasms
without gusts of wind
in mortal concentration

until the red superfluous
moon tore itself away

***UNDER A TREE WITHOUT COLOR

under a tree without color
the shape of his body

joined to it but alien
exact but dry

it breathes though not alive
it's only a reflection

you can multiply it
almost into infinity

so many correct objects
at every stop
on every strange square
under each tree of a dream

***THE EVENING CITY

the evening city
a habitat of soot

moldy windows
rust in gardens
silence of door handles

on a laundry line
a shirt ripping

at dawn
a ship sailed off

for a long time you saw
that green tree
chased by salt

***NIGHTINGALES ON THE ÎLE ST-LOUIS START UP IN MID-MARCH

nightingales on the Île St-Louis start up in mid-March
always ahead of time cloudy air trembles
what is that voice
between a sleeping mole and an unreal wing
what happens is torn from earth but doesn't fly away
nightingales in mid-March like a children's crusade
a procession along parapets under the sun's dry branch
what happens is without significance or calculation
there are neither roots nor canopy even the wind
is without memory without any future
with a scent torn from a ruin's windows and stairs
a Calvary of voices in the wasteland air
they touch where do the cages go
nightingales on the island nightingales in mid-March

***IN THE CLEARING UNDER A TREE JOHANN KASPAR LAVATER WAITED

In the clearing under a tree Johann Kaspar Lavater waited
I knew him by his *vatermörder* collar and the mildew on his lips
"Es ist schon spät wir müssen uns beeilen"
By ship? I asked. "Si" and he pointed with his cane the sun
died out the stars came close and began to hiss
We ran up the stairs where a throng of people stood barefoot
with open mouths By rats' corridors crystal ballrooms
and empty frames like gouged-out eyes all the way to the hatboxes
Lavater extended his hand I will never forget the touch
We climbed panting up a ladder made of cotton
fire following behind I saw his back and his purple vest
a fall: like someone flipping through an illustrated book
I came to by a gray ocean with my mouth full of hair
the fire lay flat on its back with its head lopped off
Lavater was smaller than usual
he paced around the coffin filling it with water plants
we boarded it and that's when the regular journey began

HAIR

In the night
hair grows
from the wall

it's not a lock
behind memory's ear

nor does it belong
to the restless lap of night

separated from skin
it lives
a dry life apart

its movements are restless
at any touch
it contracts
painfully

neither white
nor black
its color is more like
a whisper

neither gnashing of teeth
nor sudden cry
nor tearing with fingers
is capable of scaring it off

hair grows straight from the wall

FROM HERODOTUS

When the beasts of burden had given out
Cleobis Biton two brothers and athletes
got into harness The cart with a stone goddess
travels the bumpy road from Argos to Heraion

Helios urges his golden steeds on and Poseidon
makes salt waves leap like dolphins in the sea
The winds' cheeks puff up and the earth
bears fruits heavy with sweetness
Cleobis Biton draw their marble Mother on

After the heroic deed was done the gods
were asked to give the brothers the best reward
after their offering Cleobis and Biton sleep
in Hera's inner temple they sleep a stony sleep

The sculptor's name was Polymides
He didn't wake the dead he raised up their heavy bodies
cleaned them of blood and sweat wove eternity into braids
he gave their enormous eyes a grainy peace

Cleobis Biton two brothers and athletes

MR COGITO AND CERTAIN MECHANISMS OF MEMORY

I

Suddenly it seems there is nothing more fragile than a landscape
One motion of the eyelid annihilates a mountain range buries the Alps
A head turned away dries up the ocean of memory an ocean transformed
   into a lump of salt
An abandoned forest is as hard to remember as a hotel room
Only the landscape of childhood only that landscape
we carry always in the depths of all memories
its colors are muted a drawing concave as a stamp
an intense smell of roots and unexpected glimmerings shaded by an
   eyelash

II

The landscape of childhood overgrown with reeds
the landscape of youth passed by at a gallop
Through the cracks of distraction between parted legs the pages of an
   open newspaper
through a windowpane through a breath we see the landscape of maturity
All of this should fall apart someday
turn black like old decorations

fall silent like murmuring choirs
marring the pure aria of our existence

III

What happens is quite the reverse no doubt against our will
landscapes return invading our memory
repeating themselves sleeplessly whole chains of them vast herds
twilight in the orchard crooked apple trees a steep slope or a house with
   green shutters
and a black tar-paper roof (one window open)—the sun on a yellow wall
covered in grapevines the orchard the wall of the house a boat at the
   water's edge—
blue tracks running out of the forest—what flute leads them out from our
   memory
who will cut the celluloid reel

IV

It is not language at all it's wrong to draw out symbols
this is the brutal victory of a background
alien to our existence
a river took the legs a branch struck out the head
where the shoulder lay there is now a line of hills
in the place of the heart a foreign city dry as an etching

V
—

Conclusion

If it is mildew growing if the bacteria of images
multiply so fast as if we were their nourishment
and nothing more the lesson must be
write your name on tree bark
put your faith in wise stones
imprint your hand on the air and water
if that moment comes
don't clutch at the curtain
but disappear into the folds
—unreconciled to be sure

MYCENAE

Aegisthus sleeps. Walls are snoring
The blood has dried a bit on stone
Electra yawns. Five in the morning
Her shoulders weigh a heavy yoke

She descends the steps down to the cistern
with its nocturnal bat-like dampness
Before the pail disturbs the water
She sees her father's enormous eyes

filled with terror. So without a cry
Agamemnon converses with his child
All day washing. Piles of laundry
Bedclothes stained by stubborn blood

At evening a banquet. Clytemnestra
lovely as ever. It's a booze-up
Tears and laughter and tears again
A blind man plays some faltering music

The epic is ancient and worn thin
like a harrow driven over bones

in the thick darkness of the megaron
a low voice creeps across the stones

And then to speed things up a little
they carry the bodies up from below
drag them to banquet tables to funnel
wine into their nonexistent throats

There is a moment of quiet when necks
wilt from the powerful fumes of wine
the dead and the killers are reconciled
by a shade taking down a hanging axe

WORDS

They haven't had their final say

patient as the builders of the pyramids
stubborn as convicts at the Polar Circle
burnt at the stake
shot in the cellars of the Palace of Justice
they are silent

it is not words but their faint shadows
dripping from dictators' lips
blasting from megaphones
rustling like dry grass in memoranda
in newspapers

they are patient

they survived the Flood
they survived Hammurabi
they will survive brains on a leash

***DURING A SLEEPLESS NIGHT

during a sleepless night
he repeats three words

revolves them
a long time in his mind
like a rosary

they are far-flung words
do not form a sentence

the plain between them
is desolate and cold

he gets up carefully
so as not to wake his insomnia

gingerly approaches the table
where a lamp is swaying

but the journey was long
words fell by the wayside

sank deeper under the skin
melted into the bloodstream

he'll have to work long and hard
to get them back out

he'll have to speed up
his heart's rhythm
or slow it down

and maybe once again
someone will write them on a wall
in the catacombs of night
on the milky glass of dawn

MR COGITO'S ADDENDUM TO THE TRAGEDY OF MAYERLING

In the spring of 1889 my great-grandfather lost his appetite. He awoke in the night screaming. He became pathologically suspicious. He no longer trusted the Emperor, accused Count von Taaffe of the most dreadful things, feared the jealous Mizzi Kaspar, and said of the coachman Bratfisch and the butler Loschek that they would do anything for money.

My great-grandfather loved Maria Vetsera with a great, hidden and hopeless passion. Under the gray uniform of the private court counselor a fire raged that he did not wish to extinguish.

Bent as if over an Easter cake, without wrath or elation, my great-grandmother plunges a large kitchen knife into Maria Vetsera's beautiful body.

Who could have foreseen that at that very moment my great-grandfather's heart, weary beyond all measure, would stop, thereby joining itself to the dark tragedy of the fall of the empire.

MR COGITO AND THE TASKS OF ART

Everything that can be achieved
by so-called art
is contained in the concept of reconciliation

it isn't a reconciliation with power
or with life
understood as daily torment

it's significantly deeper
a reconciliation with things

to make the sunrise
impossible to bear

a mountain
higher than a mountain

to restore terror
that is to say beauty

in other words
to make life
worthy of life

and if possible
if at all possible
season it with disagreement
beautiful disproportion

the uncertainty of reality yes
uncertainty

ANGELS OF CIVILIZATION

At the turn of the century it seemed that angels would leave us for good and that no trace would remain of them. They were still employed here and there by funeral directors. They also propped up old-fashioned canopies. But in fact they grew pale from idleness and gradually turned into pink powder.

The true renaissance of angels came with the development of airlines. It can be said without exaggeration that angels returned to earth and took on the flush of life. They help us pass across a footbridge suspended high above the oceans. From the loudspeakers of airports their high unreal voices seep unctuously as if they wish to persuade us there is still some rescue.

They speak all languages, but they have the same smile for heavenly ascension and catastrophe.

CAT (II)

It can be any sort, really: the feral Roman red with patchy fur and a scarred nose like a veteran of Caesar's legions that I tried in vain to coax out of the ruins of the Forum Romanum.

Or that untamed black giant in Pasadena that tried to warn me of the imminent earthquake and not being understood, vanished for good, leaving me in murky ignorance about the oceans, stars and volcanoes.

Or the familiar sort, born in a barn amid flowering meadows of hay, floods of urine and gentle hillocks of flesh fragrant with milk.

It can be any sort: any cat whatsoever is an unfathomed soul, who doesn't hover over shimmering waters but walks the path of solitary sages on four soft paws.

KNOT

MONOM/K/E'S C/P

When Mr Cogito grows into a dignified old age, he will not collect stamps, ancient coins or rare books. He will establish the world's first collection of knots. He will make efforts to persuade others of the charms of the mysteries of knots.

People have never given knots their due. Nor have they learned to admire the complexities of their beauty. They have chopped through knots with swords like that Macedonian idiot, or simply disentangled them, proud that they now have the odious string, fit to tie a piglet to a tree or fling around a loved one's throat.

MONOMAKH'S CAP

There used to be a single cap. Just as it should be. Now—they say—there are many of them in each district. And they're all alike—they say—carefully hidden under a patch of burdock, mixed in with the manure and gnawed bones, so no one will fawn over them.

Why anyone wants them, God only knows. But apparently there are still those who smile at them in their dreams—at that twisted wire, material faded as an old bandage, adorned with a stolen pearl.

There used to be one. Just as it should be. And everyone knew what was what. But now we don't know who will have life, and who, death.

MR COGITO'S DREAM

he began to walk faster
clutching in a moist hand
a page torn from a notebook
with a list of shopping

buy
string
four blessed candles
a kilogram of feathers
for a quilt for his aunt
who died in winter
and is now freezing

          nothing there

buy
a key
a window fitting
a fitting for a door

       houses were bathed
       in a deathlike glow

buy
a clock
chrysanthemums

     darkness rolled
     from the rooftops

buy
a chain
Amphitheatrum Sapientiae Aeternae
verbena
vinegar

     Now he was almost running
     the hour was nearing
     when the shops close
     the eyelids slam shut

MR COGITO'S
DREAM-AWAKENING

She went with a step still as a spring
she was dressed in a gown of pebbles
in a birch tree in the bark of morning
dawn went on the right and on the left
a path and so went—time and place

it wasn't I who shouted and—rejected—
fell into waking so that I now search
with a cane for matches a sweaty hand
among medications sleeping pills
and her afterimage in my vacant eyes
rustles like poppy seed smells of rope

FROM MR COGITO'S EROTICA

First lady of my fingers empress of my hair
mistress of the pain points on my vast skin
Angel of the rib taken from me by stealth
as I slept my shoulder bones folded like wings

      on the long chord of my innards
      on the black throat of my hunger
      on my lungs' pipes belly's drum
      lies an elliptical stone of silence

I draw you in snagged on the line of my dream
an ant's touch opens the body's loose burrow
from this moment our breath will rise as one
from the vertiginous pinnacle of the spine

FROM THE FIRM'S HISTORY (JUNE 1976)

For Lech Bądkowski

It now looked as if it was really over and our Firm, which for years had bravely battled adversities of fate, would announce its demise. Production had sunk to sea level, the coffers were empty, the only thing left to be sold on the market was potting soil.

Things were gloomy, cave-like, but without a cave-like faith in progress. Slender electric energy reserves were barely sufficient to light sad official funerals at even sadder conventions.

Everywhere discontent was expressed in strikes. The streets swarmed with crowds. The directors lost their heads.

And then the unfailing Guard was sent out—the Firm's rubber arm. It acted efficiently, with a sense of mission, knowing well that what is small and concrete must be sacrificed for great matters like Andromeda's nebula. So all you heard was the measured threshing of truncheons. Stifled cries. Finally, silence.

Before long everything was back to normal. Yet again our Firm had emerged unscathed, had overcome obstacles, and proudly stepped into a new era. Far-reaching reforms were announced. Excessively sluggish shorthand secretaries were let go and a few accountants with bright ideas were brought in. There was the promise of raises.

But no one, not even the greatest optimists, expected things to be this good. A color TV was purchased for the break room.

On the glass screen we can once again watch our directors, who happily recovered their lost heads. They're a bit blue in the face, but alive, resourceful—and as it would appear, irreplaceable.

FROM AN UNWRITTEN THEORY OF DREAMS

IN MEMORY OF JEAN AMÉRY

I

The torturers sleep soundly their dreams are rosy
good-natured genocides—foreign and home-grown
already forgiven by brief human memory
a gentle breeze turns the pages of family albums
the windows of the house open to August the shade of an apple tree in
    bloom
under which a noble brood has gathered
grandfather's open carriage an expedition to church
first communion mother's first embrace
a campfire in a clearing and a starry sky
without omens or mysteries without an Apocalypse
so they sleep soundly their dreams are wholesome
full of food drink fleshy bodies of women
with whom to play erotic games in bushes in groves
and over all of this floats a forgotten voice
a voice pure as a spring innocent as an echo
singing of a boy who spied a rose on the heath

memory's bell awakens no ghosts or nightmares
memory's bell repeats its great absolution

they wake in the early morning full of will and strength
carefully they shave their bourgeois cheeks
what remains of their hair they style as a laurel wreath
in the waters of oblivion that wash all away
they lather their bodies with soap of the brand *Macbeth*

2

Why does sleep—the shelter of all human beings—
withhold its favor from the victims of violence
why do they bleed at night between clean sheets
and go to their beds as if they were torture chambers
cells on death row or the shadow of the gallows
after all they too had mothers and they have seen
the forest clearing sky blossoming apple tree rose
who drove all this from every corner of their souls
they too experienced moments of happiness so why
does their howling awaken the innocent household
why do they tear off yet again on their mad escape
beating their heads on a wall then sleep no more
staring dully at the clock that won't change a thing

memory's bell repeats its great terror
memory's bell beats an unceasing alarm

true it's hard to admit that torturers won the victory
the victims have now been vanquished for all eternity

so they must make terms with this punishment without guilt
with the scar of shame the fingermarks on their cheeks

the abject will to survive—the temptation of forgiveness
the story of hell is now rightly felt to be in bad taste

there's no longer any place to lodge a complaint
the tribunal of dreams delivers unfathomable verdicts

GENERATION

between us a secret pact like an undeclared love
neighboring dates of birth crippling experience

there's no way to explain it rationally

all of us volunteers in the cruel war called literature
we knew it only from holy pictures and false reports
you do penance for lightheartedness as you do for crime
you pay

we fooled ourselves that we'd be the vanguard
that we'd open the road to the promised land
we quickly lost contact with man's regular army

> on the desk of memory Paul lays ten
> helpless fingers then folds them
> into an artful braid he's silent—as if
> fleeing across the Red Sea
> or plumbing the mussel-clad depths of the Seine
> Ingeborg in Deianira's shirt burns forever with a cigarette
> on her red lips—Marian in a skid row hotel
> in Paris carefully counts out
> his hoarded tablets of eternal sleep

with the focus of a sprinter John takes a run-up
on the Washington Avenue Bridge and long-faced Sylvia
as if reflected in a wave in a cloud of gas fumes
prophecies—a poor abandoned Pythia

some have chosen a *soi-disant* natural demise
Günter Bruno his face on the Olympia typewriter
like an artilleryman killed on a gun carriage
The heart of Tadeusz exploded with rapture
when he found the word he'd stalked for years
Janos was crucified on a white sheet of paper

before long I'll be alone it's a bitter winter
a great white surface of snow black forest
my shako pushed back epaulets hoarfrost
a useless sword and two pistols
made by Conny & Brown

I struggle not to envy the dead
though I know what awaits me
death at the hands of shady figures
who will have taken a fancy
to my silver buttons

and at that moment
in a place on earth unknown
someone will start shaping
innocent words of hope

OUR CHILD

Our test-tube child is developing beautifully
a blue-eyed lad a pink Futurus
spared measles whooping cough scarlet fever
bed-wetting and fear of the big bad witch
he loved UFOs—they winked at him affably

When he was three he developed senile dementia
so his head was replaced in the same factory
where he first saw the light soon he returned to us
and raucously played with a robot in the sitting room

He was taken on by an astute analyst of the soul
(more precisely of the hole called soul by Plato)
Our son's IQ beat all previous records
and the sprat soon became a world champion of tests
being wealthy people we didn't give him to a circus
he's our child after all even if he's from a test tube
one TV appearance and that would be the end of it

Gifted as the young Pascal groundbreaking like Einstein
he doesn't attend school because he might get a complex
he studies on his own writes and listens to Eastern music
which facilitates a grasp of extra-rational connections

When he was twelve he published several books
they immediately made the bestseller list
reviewers praised the capital syntheses
comparing Marx to Buddha Christ to Talleyrand
the malicious faulted him for conceptual confusion
but our son had liberated himself from all concepts

One thing troubles us that he is rather melancholy
and frequently succumbs to fits of irritation
you can't use certain words or expressions around him
such as God conscience or the nation
for then he will stamp his feet and block his ears
on the other hand he is invariably amused by funerals
wars plagues famine

Our test-tube son will become a professor
he's waiting for a suitable department to be set up
he's working on a system that he christened Presentism
which boldly rejects all ontology
crumbling categories of time and space
a few other minor matters
                              put very simply
it's a philosophy of the instant of moments unconnected
to each other or to the cosmos an apology for chance
in other words for absolute freedom

when nothingness sends its luminous signals
and another nothingness answers with booming laughter

SLEEP'S DECORATIONS

Always cities not a trace of the sea
nor a forest green meadow or desert
only houses and squares alleys and outskirts

an intolerable confusion of cities: Siena
traversed by Piotrkowska Street London mixed up
with Rome—suddenly without warning Tottenham Court Road breaks off
and via Dandolo begins leading up the hill

always hybrids though for years I tortured my memory
and trained my eye so that I can summon up and draw
churches towers and cityscapes seen long ago

perhaps my sleep is patiently reminding me
of my betrayals escapes sundering of ties
fickleness of heart

or it's simply telling me that I am an exile
who was denied a house in the valley
a clock on a tower eternal time

      magnificent human space eternal time

***MY POOR KINGDOM
I STILL DEFEND YOU

My poor kingdom I still defend you
I mend the low wall stormed by the invader
build barricades of earth though I have no army

no one looks this way but those who will kill me
yet I make every effort to keep it looking good
straight gravel-strewn paths a green bower

and also an oak and a pine and bronze beeches
summer blossoms and meadow insects and birds
a garden snake an owl a comical hedgehog

I could have surrendered ages ago or fled by night
but I still defend you I myself don't know why
like a pitiful king on an ancient coin

my poor kingdom the kingdom of doubt

ON THE DAY OF JUDGMENT

On the Day of Judgment
angels bellow like hustlers of fate on Omonia Square
thick crowds throng up and down in all directions
(the ride upward or downward is to begin in a moment
mothers lose their children fathers their families and heads
it's as if the last train were departing from a besieged city

in a sky the color of a Texas sunset
writing appears on walls in an entirely impenetrable language
at times a bolt of lightning strikes but its voice is lost in the mob
angels bellow clobber people on the head
there's no order at all
humanity is incorrigible

industry has come to a standstill but trade is flourishing

MR COGITO AND UTOPIAS

Usually on an island The sea's blue net
fends off foreign influences and so the rootless flower
grows tall on the sands of reason

High walls though those who dwell here
never admit there are other worlds
if there is perfection
it must be singular

So there are no rebellions here
no wealth or poverty
straight streets
houses all the same
children are born
old people die
from a high tower
the bell tolls us
to sleep

the rest is work

They've driven from the sunny state all shadows
scorpions secrets torments conscience
the one deity keeps a golden silence without promises

Philosophers govern for in truth they know
all there is to know about original sin warped nature
the hell of dreams and the hell of freedom

So they built a city
a city without history
no ancestral shades here
no delusion of paradise
no shadow of a hope

Chronicles relate that a man once
escaped from utopia
at night he knocked together a raft
and the sea whisked him off to the real earth

No one will tell us with what trepidation
this citizen of utopia observed
the lives of other people
their private property their wars commerce and rebellions
freaks of fate percentage of capital
above all
that everyone was separate
as a world
or a comet

but he soon got used to it he made a great fortune by usury of course
built a house with a garden married a fat woman

had mistresses a bunch of children appliances he didn't need
he exhausted his slaves drank a lot played at knucklebones
simply lived a human life

but agents of utopia agents on the mainland
captured him and took him back to his native isle
to meet his punishment

he was flayed of his skin and died a lingering death
lashed to a pole outside the city walls

Utopias are on the rise more of them all the time
on inaccessible islands behind a great wall of water
or stone or mere barbed wire

The only hope then is for the world to burst out laughing
and lay waste to the city of the sun on the sands of reason
so that later an archaeologist may admire the straight streets
the sewers the ruins of the tower the philosophers' palace
the houses that are all the same and the obedient bones

***THAT LITTLE HAND ON THE WHITE SHEET

That little hand on the white sheet
its fine bones clothed in skin they lie
they feign life clenched into a fist
they fight for a moment more above the abyss

this little hand deserves tenderness
raise it up to your mouth like a microphone
saying perfidies meetings at the station
events without grace and dreams without symbols

this little hand lives on its own strength
as if a gust of brightness drove it here
from the dead island of the body

it hesitates in the middle of the sheet then thoughtfully almost
reluctantly expresses its consent to rigor
and takes on a ghostly transparency

CONTRA AUGUSTINUM PONTIFICEM IN TERRA NUBICA PECCATOREM IN PURGATORIO

A saint after all. Bishop of Hippo. A flame.
White with heat he writes in a concise style
with a seductive pen of fire sentences of fire
and above all the blasphemous
ama et fac quod vis

For centuries it will be the battle cry
of the violent. Of those who pass lightly on a plank over the abyss
of those who pass from a tender whisper
to the clatter of centurions roar of battle roar of the slain

He won't retract that sentence now. In vain
the anxious silence of synods the oath in the wind
the efforts of scholarchs to salvage something at least

Therefore we who in the same school of crimes committed from good
    intentions
learned gradations—dark—darker—nothingness
bright—bright—exaltation

let us pray for him.

A STONE IN JERUSALEM

Indifferent
to the fate
of my mortal remains

utterly
indifferent
to the fate
of the manuscripts
I leave in disorder

I would like
if it is not
too great
an honor
to have a grave
in Jerusalem

among
olive trees
other stones
on a hill
at the mercy
of the sun

may
David
my patient teacher
of the prophets' tongue
appear
by grace
at the funeral
and also Yehuda
poet
lion of Judah

my brother
Dan won't come
because he died
and so is near me
in eternity

and also
a few friends from Poland

I ask for
a Kaddish
in the tongue
of my ancestors
by my friend Al
may he say it
from memory by grace

the poet Rühmkopf from Hamburg
may he read
a poem

in his cold
studio
on the top floor
of an ugly building

the poet Joseph Brodsky
may he be of good cheer
and wish me peace

may Kasia—who was true to me—
give alms to Saint Anna of God
to feed the poor
because in my life
I didn't do so
often enough

I think I've left no one out

***I'M LOOKING FOR THE POEMS OF DAN PAGIS

I'm looking for the poems of Dan Pagis
—They're probably in the desert now
They've been spotted between the oasis El-Djabel
and the port of Eilat

In Czernowitz they must be on every street corner

Universally Unavailable

like the sermon of the storm
the hush of many waters
the diamond heart of the hummingbird

TRENCHES

Those buried knee-deep in their forefathers

You wouldn't give up utopia it was too nourishing seductive
For mommy's boys the heirs of fortune heirs
To the bloody myths of the twentieth century

Your paltry triumphs—the death of the gods of copybook headings
Pyramids of chaos concentrated misery
Burning provinces of death camps and cold Siberian bunks

The twilight of the fraudsters is upon us but still unborn
The bookkeeper of the era in spectacles of barbed wire
Who swears alternately in Russian and in German

> In forests and cities they will leave behind trenches
> From the terrible battle for man's soul where sedges
> Now plant their green banner in a true wind

> Ants crawl blindly across these pits of crime
> Rain splashes rocking their nothingness
> So not even a field mouse will move in here

> Old men disappoint no one now listens to their song of necessity
> Or their maledictions from beyond the grave and so for all eternity
> They will dwell alone in the valley of scorn

TO MICHAEL KRÜGER

1

In the end I came to like you my mortal enemies
inherited like an illness poverty a bad back
the road was long from the trenches to the tavern
so I came to like you Michael
and you Hubert Gunther Horst Nikolaus and Werner Jan—a long list
Barbara—Sybilla—Renata—Eleonora—
there's no sentimentality in this
no games cunning seduction
there's only great astonishment
      I have forgotten nothing
      I lack the power to forgive
      I don't wish to let myself off lightly
      those who were killed
      remain killed forever
      a house turned into rubble
      the taste of ash and revenge
      and yet you and I have gone out
      for a mug of beer
      in green gardens with white chairs
      when lindens scatter
      their sweet sticky seeds

and we spoke of the banality of evil
the twists of fate
freaks of fortune
and it was a great astonishment
a pitiless joy

2

the sky waters hills
are just the same
mothers push their prams
elders go under the ground
a handful of youths
still study violence
your men
amazingly hardworking
pure
now fall asleep
cautiously
deeply
and without nightmares
two generations
and everything is different
the actors
the set
the drama
I did nothing
—alien to me were
the hiccup of reconciliation
the bargaining in the cemetery

discussions
back and forth like billiard balls
I wandered
from city to city
smiled at girls
chatted interminably
in trains
at night
in hallways
guest rooms
on boats
under Lorelei's scale
in opera foyers
in administrative buildings
I did nothing
I wished merely to understand

3

I write this in a house
on the Starnberger See
the last king of Bavaria
was cruelly drowned here
now the swans
weep for him
from three windows
arched as in a chapel
you can see a November forest
supple branches
thickly set needles

the color of copper
as in the old tapestry
Hunt for the Unicorn
the lake wavers
between darkness
and deep blue metal
on the horizon the Alps
like a ripped-up score by Wagner
for whom I honestly—God is my witness—
never cared
it's all unreal
and beautiful
as the laughter of the gods
the larches outside the window
sing softly
sudden storms occur here
and then everything is
heavy
brown
and dark blue
or a mountain wind
comes in
and then everything is surreal
painfully self-evident
covered in a shining glaze
perhaps everything that happened between us
—what do you think Michael—
is simply
the meteorology of emotions

but a certain courage was required
to bring oneself to make the gesture
a half turn of the body
to look one another in the eye

MR COGITO'S DISABILITY

1

everything
but literally everything
should incline Mr Cogito
to pass over in silence
to conceal
his Great Disability

no one
apart from God
should know about it

neither friend
nor treacherous lover
nor spymaster night

now
he has decided
on a confession
fraught with consequences

he knows
that his days are numbered
and each of us would like to die
cleansed
without taint
a powerful instinct
impels him to give testimony
as a person
on his deathbed
confesses to killing
basely cheating an old lady
betraying his country

2

confession:

Mr Cogito
was born
lived
and will depart
as an individual
COMPLETELY DEVOID OF A SUBCONSCIOUS

so he was
a changeling
a freak of nature
like a bearded lady
a two-headed calf
a child without limbs

for years
with great grief and pain
he concealed
his terrible handicap
he lied
like others
bored his family
saying that he had a Narcissus syndrome
that his dreams were full of ladders and swords
and that he had an overwhelming desire
to kill his father

like others
he fell victim
to frauds in white coats
equipped with a single scientific tool
a couch
upholstered in black oilskin

like the one at Berggasse
number 19

3
—

but now
he's bored by
evasions
masquerades
social mimicry

he'd very much like
to stand in the market square
before City Hall and the Lord on High
and confess at the top of his voice
that he never had a subconscious

When on hot August afternoons
in the Bois de Boulogne
he felt a passionate yearning
for artificial ice
that same night
in his dreams
there appeared cones of plenty
filled with Antarctic glaciers of vanilla
red as cherries
green as his favorite pistachio

relatives and loved ones
stood quietly at the bed
disappeared
without complaint
and left Mr Cogito
with the painful certainty
that they were beyond the reach
of his pity
love
recompense

Mr Cogito
secretly envied those
who as soon as they drop off

turn into werewolves
sadists emperors
heroic prisoners of the state

he feels an envy beyond words
for those who after a killer day
have enough strength
enough imagination
to spin out of nothing

absurd edifices
Baroque symbols
funfair nightmares

EPILOGUE TO THE TEMPEST

I

the ship is sailing off you can still catch a glimpse
it's like a hare bounding through the sea's thick grass
I took advantage of the confusion and stayed behind
with you Caliban I gave up my title of King of Naples
for the honor of being the first citizen of this island
You Caliban will be the people all rolled into one
I hope we will found an ideal state

I'm sure Alonso will pick a quarrel with Antonio
at the very first pretext or without any at all
over that worm-eaten apple the Kingdom of Naples
and whoever is quicker will cut his brother's throat
and then others will start killing each other blindly
betraying instigating revolt weaving nets of intrigue
which is to say making history so Clio may write
burn write again and falsify the book for posterity
the history of the struggle of black ants against red
Gonzalo will probably die in a dungeon
Ferdinand and Antonio gnaw at each other like rats
Trinculo the clown will go completely off his rocker
it's not inconceivable that the ship will reach Naples

empty not counting Trinculo who left with the captain
the boatswain and other sailors after the bloodbath
will be ordinary and stink like the bottom of a cask
                    This isn't for us Caliban
whom our thrice glorious patron once called a *savage*
misshapen knave I think he did you an injustice
I always felt you had a good heart and common sense
and in these times they are worth their weight in gold
whereas people

2

Oh I forgot to say that on the island
total pantheism reigns and just as in Plato
so with us everything has its ideal form its place in the Pantheon
so there's a goddess of the morning star and also a god of the left foot
a goddess of the jaguar's death a deity of the apple blossom
and another one for the fruit—this is why our poets never fall
ill and do not rustle words like withered grass

today I wrote a short psalm to a teardrop
sing it for me Caliban in the side altar of pines
and remember to bust out the silver soprano
you keep so jealously under your Adam's apple
for special occasions
                    O look at the sky
the wind's graceful fingers are weaving cirrus clouds
as if made of pink wool let us praise the divine cirrus
every wind that is born and every wind that is silent

3

The island is ours Caliban—the ebb and flow of the sea
fogs and earthquakes the sun's swelter and the night's chill
we will be cradled by the elements that's the main thing
the important things are water fire the abysses of heaven
and the abysses of blue

—I think you'll agree with me Caliban
our system will be simple
you will govern on the even dates and I on the uneven
we'll establish the most noble form of government:
lying belly up Now
on religion for it's the most important thing

—we timidly believe in the soul's immortality
because how would we cope otherwise
This should not be an obstacle in our striving
toward a life of virtue and moderate austerity

THE REALITY OF EVIL

no particular marks none of the features proper to objects
that's why it's so devious that the honorable senses pass by
indifferently don't sound the alarm

       that'll be where the rotten apple of Eden came in
neither good nor evil in fact but round as Newton's universe
and also the heavy chains of symbols and prophetic signs
of the underworld beast tarry thorns the smell of sulfur
demons of day and night to cough up that horrible old truth
that evil is concrete as a table or a moon

       we don't know if it is a living being or a crystal
perfectly divisible no horde of rats or bacteria cancer cells
can compete with its ability to multiply
evil becomes visible only when it crosses an unknown boundary
it irritates the nostrils and the eye

       it is everywhere sometimes still hidden
in a child's clenched fists in a rainbow in the scents of spring
in a sunny apparition in the call of a quail

seen by the crucified Manes Augustine Origen
       the prophets

therefore be careful like deer in a clearing
in a wood full of wolves when you go to drink
don't be lured
by sweet sunshine by gusts of wind murmuring in the leaves

MANDELSTAM

In the end like all great poets he became a jester
at the court of mosses and lichens in the sovereign kingdom of the tundra
he prompts general hilarity when on all fours like a dog
he searches for scraps of food *wiechno nienazhraty**

So for the amusement of prisoners comrades in slavery the poet crows
like a rooster turns somersaults does handstands
and when invention fails him he simply plays the Jew

Decades have passed now no one is looking for you
unless in the other world Mr Brodsky now searches for a trace
he was always so precise space and time abandoned him
he counted syllables like a miser but also conversed with shades

And Mandelstam dances for the amusement of the *urkas*
in terror's deadly nightshirt his face pelted with apple cores
forgotten on the bottom of the Red Sea
which closed over his head he will not see Jerusalem

And Mandelstam dances to increase the joy of existence
Mandelstam dances barefoot in the snow alone

---

*   Russ. eternally underfed

SPRING (FROM THREE
EROTIC POEMS)

We sit across from each other
in the high grass
our bare feet touching

the props of spring
have discreetly withdrawn

so that we may
in silence
one on one
perform our ritual
of touching bare feet
to the point of distraction

I pray
for her to be silent
just for a moment
silent

each reckless word
may awaken
the monster of time

and then
everything will transform
into motion and forgetting

so I implore God
for her to be silent
so that we may go on playing
love's tournament of bare feet

may she wait just a moment
before she intones
her sorrow
over the broken pitcher

before she starts to circle
like a lost fledgling
the disaster
of her vanquished fortress

let it last
the blessed scent of sweat
the look of oblivion
the tousled hair
the undone buttons
and thoughts

WINTER (FROM THREE EROTIC POEMS)

I now think
disgracefully rarely
of my First Great Abandoned One

I carefully avoid
anything that might cause
a consternation of memories
—places we used to meet
—street corners
—landscapes
—benches
—trees
—the window where
our light burned

slowly but pitilessly
I forget
the color of her eyes

what
remains
now rests
in a cardboard box

photographic negatives
our faceless pictures
if someone ran a pointer finger
down the sharp edge of the frame
the heart's blood
would flow

    a friend told me
    that My First Great Love
    now lives alone
    not counting the sea's company

    she is blind
    and occupies herself with weaving

    what does she weave
    on the dark loom

    for me it's like
    an empty platform

    like absolute
    irrevocability

    like a pensive drowned man
    with a hat firmly jammed
    over his ears

who floats
with his head turned away
from the world

like night
in a mirror

HAGIOGRAPHIC-
ZOOLOGICAL MEDITATIONS
OF MR COGITO

I

Next to Saint Patrick
Mr Cogito's favorite saint
is Francis of Assisi

alone among
attendants of the Throne
this intimate of the Almighty
stood up for
the speechless

(in Assisi
his cloak is on display
a coarse
woven sack
covering
a tortured body
a burning heart
a frail poverty)

the only one
who stood up

for all
slaughtered
strangled
bled out
sacrifices
to our pride

he is portrayed
with birds
perched
on his arms
as on the branches
of a tree

2

—but does your saint's
affection extend to cats
asks a faux naif
Satan
Mr Cogito's tempter

—are you not incited
by the serpent of hypocrisy
the mincing postures
of the friend
of all Creation

Mr Cogito knows very well
that since he started to share

bed and board
with a cat
the fowl of the air have deserted him

the friendly doves
as well as
starlings
titmice
even sparrows
have flown off
never to return

Mr Cogito would like to call out
like golden-toothed Father Jankowski
like golden-tongued Father Rydzyk
Get thee behind me Satan
Get thee behind me Tempter

but these exorcisms
don't do the slightest
bit of good

once sown
the seed of doubt
gnaws the conscience
gives him no peace

because honestly for when it comes down to it
hand on heart
does Mr Cogito love
all animals equally

the lion and the antelope
the wolf and the lamb
the snake and the nightingale

here too there's nothing democratic
about love

again we have
varying degrees
gradations
hypocrisy's wiles

who can truly love
the live crocodile
(glove manufacturers
love it dead)
let alone the hyena

3

Mr Cogito is disturbed
by the lack of a clear
either-or

the lack of legible criteria

Is only what is small
and fluffy
deserving of love

what to do about the hippopotamus
a sympathetic character
after all

perhaps if we dried him off
lit him well
and scoured him

but not wet
and slippery

on the other hand
what to do with the shark the barracuda
or the most magnificent
dolphin

the lack of clear-cut
Kantian
categories
erodes Mr Cogito's love
for the animal world

(in his youth
he read Brehm)

the whole matter
must be thought through
examined
from a theological
phenomenological
and every other scientific angle

but for now
Mr Cogito
scatters
crumbs in the birdless
garden
with on his shoulder
his favorite
the tomcat Shu-shu

BREVIARY. TRIFLES

Lord, I give thanks to you for small daily cares, small worries, disorder creeping from matter to mind, from which one must defend oneself

—for helping me pick a tie to fit my shirt so I now look like an urbane hangman
—for helping me find a matching sock
—and helping me shave the patch of particularly stubborn hair under my nose so that I could take another step forward in my quest for beauty

Be praised Lord that you determined that things as tiny as capillary veins are connected with important things and that in the end I don't know myself how to classify my injured left leg—it's a nuisance but without it I wouldn't have stood at the graves of fallen friends to rest and reflect

Be praised Lord and receive my gratitude for my insomnia, from which I suffer and which also benefits me, because it opens up before me the abyss of time, summons from memory events and people I would have long forgotten if not for the miracle of insomnia, without which I would sleep the sleep of the righteous, who are worthy of respect but also a bit dull

I thank You—that you created my world of threads, ribbons, buttons, sewing goods, common ideas and despite this, or rather because of it, I beheld in these trifles Your countenance

UNTITLED

FOR BARBARA TORUŃCZYK

I

My God,
     how terribly I loved him
     more than my father or Mama
     more than the Polish Army or vanilla ice cream
     he always went
     a half step behind me
     I felt on my back his warm breath
     I heard his wings brush each other
     delicately and softly as if
     two silk ribbons were starting a conversation
     I prayed to him as to a God
     all children suffer from polytheism
     I never looked at him
     he was not given to me as a sense impression
     rather he was a state of consciousness
     although in fact on the basis
     of material proofs (a holy picture memento of my first communion)
     I knew what he looked like
     a tall blue-eyed blond
     with a star on his forehead
     he led me along a narrow plank

above the ravine
so I loved him
I strongly believed we would be together
my whole life from the birth cry
to the sudden and unexpected—

2

Right away
when war broke out
he evaporated

yes evaporated
I have no other way
of putting it

I asked my peers

they confirmed
it was the same with them

one morning
right at the outbreak of the war
I simply ascertained
his absence
without leave

he evaporated
like a fragrance from an empty bottle

like an overexposed photograph
on which
there were supposed to be the High Castle
a meadow and
my grandmother under a colorful parasol

like the imprint
of a head on the pillow
real
and unfathomable

like a lost
identity card
proof of a vaccination for chickenpox

3

I asked my peers
the same happened to them

they explained
that right at the start of the war
their guardian angels
were summoned
to headquarters

all of them
—you understand—
all without exception
—recalled

but the worst thing was
not the lack of an angel
but the fact that
I accepted that lack
without rebellion
without a single tear of grief

he had been—now he wasn't
I loved him—I stopped loving

4
—

I remember all of this
toward the end of the day
toward the end of the century of disgrace

in a planned suburb
in a charming pub
Under the Combatant
in the orangerie of dirt

at a zinc-topped bar
bent over a glass
of oblivion

those like me
come here
white-haired boys from the forest

they mutter something
senseless
gesticulate
swear
just to fill the void with chatter

we are like the proverbial baby
thrown out with the bathwater

like whitewashed graves
like a body under cement

the owner
of Under the Combatant
burly and a bit of a braggart
with the face of an eternal corporal
glowers at me

or rather not at me
but at my glass

and when I drink the dregs
of the water of oblivion
he makes sure to top me up

he knows that people like me
pay for everything

and so he tops me up
from a great big bottle

he tops me up although
I didn't order anything

he edges up to me
moving like a cat
silent and indifferent
you hear how the sirens
of both his amputated legs
sing melodiously

suddenly
a virtuous resolution
that this is the last glass
and at the same time the certainty
it won't be the last

at the end
of the seance if
I'm lucky tonight

something will appear
in spite of everything
something will loom up
something will remind me vaguely
hushed as the voice of silk

and it may be a delusion
for I feel more than see
that someone waves a hand at me
from the last platform
of reality

then at the end of the seance
at Under the Combatant
if I'm very lucky

among
the surviving soldiers
of the regiment of the baby thrown out
with the bathwater

amid the acrid smoke
and the drunken banter

something will
return

he appears
looming
        he remembers
reminds me of something
in a hushed voice of silk

as if someone gave me a hand signal
from the last platform of the universe

MIRON

I didn't know Miron well he entered my life just once
in the electric tram on the route from Otwock to Warsaw Central
He didn't even say hello just asked me sharply if I had a valid ticket
I said yes and he said "Give it to me then" I go "What if they check?"
"Then you'll get a fine I don't even have enough for a ticket
where would I get enough for a fine." I gave him my ticket
and to the end I'll think without false modesty: it was for poetry

Once I was told he was gravely ill in bed at 55 Lwowska Street
                    first building
on the left don't knock just push the door handle
I go in it's quiet I sat on a stool that looked like a crippled centaur
from the First World War navy blankets over the windows dark
I brought everything necessary to someone who's gravely ill
a bottle of bathtub booze corked with cob the latest issue
of *People's Tribune* The air smelled of cabbage stew
the aromas of the East more precisely the Eastern Station
the smell of a pigeon that expired on the windowsill

To make him laugh I blurted out "Artur died—that
acrobat of metaphor and administration" "That's good,
that's very good" a voice from the straw mattress against the wall
or actually two voices Miron's voice pure as a spring

and the rasping voice of the Demiurg of the "Badly Shaven"
with a collar of congealed soap behind the ear
I know Artur didn't like Miron: "Never pays his dues doesn't come
to meetings takes our grants while others slog away like oxen"
—"You pays your money and you takes your choice"—I wanted to say
but something stopped me. Lady Cabbage kept spreading her odor
around the dead pigeon on the windowsill the aromas of the East
or more precisely the Eastern Station

Never in life did we speak—nor are we likely to after—
of beauty of God or the scarcity of paper
I'm proud I knew him it'll go in my memoirs it's worth preserving
for let's be honest—not everyone can say they've met an Angel

END

Day is ending Father's in the library darkness devours
the bridges capillary veins and glass-topped tables
Father gathers the ashes of it all on a newspaper
and slowly pours them into the funereal ashtray

Watching over the ceremony like a guard Aunt Pelagia
patroness of islands and remains she foretells the future
murky knotty O Father's silver head hundred-foil Pelagia

CONVERSATION

Where are you spending eternity?
I don't know. Maybe in the sand of a nebula.

BIBLIOGRAPHY

PLAYS

The Philosophers' Cave: First radio production on December 9, 1957, on Teatr Polskiego Radia. First staged production on February 6, 1961, at Teatr Dramatyczny, Warsaw. English-language production on April 2, 1963, on BBC Three.

    in the African interior there are tribes: In Herbert's original text this read "Asian interior," which was taken as a reference to the Soviet Union; the Polish censors required this to be changed. The other changes demanded included the final remarks by the Keeper of Remains about the class struggle, understood as a parody of contemporary state ideological rhetoric.

Reconstruction of the Poet: First radio production on October 7, 1960, on Teatr Polskiego Radia. First staged production on February 6, 1961, at Teatr Dramatyczny, Warsaw. English-language production on October 14, 1964, on BBC Three.

    the twentieth century by Evans: Herbert writes extensively on Arthur Evans, the British archaeologist who discovered the Minoan site of Knossos on Crete, in the essay "Labyrinth on the Sea" (*Collected Prose* 397–439).

The Other Room: First radio production on March 15, 1958, on Teatr Polskiego Radia. First staged production on May 30, 1958, at Teatr Propozycji, Bydgoszcz. Also performed with *The Philosophers' Cave* and *Reconstruction of the Poet* at Teatr Dramatyczny Warsaw, on February 6, 1961. English-language production on August 2, 1962, on BBC Three. (Translation by Halina Carroll-Najder.)

UNCOLLECTED POEMS

"Golden Mean": Published in *Dziś i Jutro*, no. 37, September 1950, along with the poems "Farewell to September" and "Inscription."

****"Fingers spindles of sound cause of melody": Published in *Tygodnik Powszechny*, no. 51/52, December 1950.

    Jerzy Zawieyski: 1902–1969, born Henryk Nowicki, a playwright, prose writer, activist, and actor whom Herbert befriended in the late 1940s and with whom he carried on an extensive correspondence.

"Pacific I": Published in ". . . I must choose every moment," in *An Almanac of Poetry*. Warsaw, PAX, 1954.

"Pacific II": Published in ". . . I must choose every moment," in *An Almanac of Poetry*. Warsaw, PAX, 1954.

"Two Stanzas": Published in *Tygodnik Powszechny*, no. 53, December 1950.

"Fra Angelico: The Martyrdom of Saints Cosma and Damian": Published in *Tygodnik Powszechny*, no. 19, 1951.

"De Profundis": Published in *Tygodnik Powszechny*, no. 40, October 1951.

"Church": Published in ". . . I must choose every moment," in *An Almanac of Poetry*. Warsaw, PAX, 1954.

"Epic": Published in the first edition of Herbert's debut collection, *Chord of Light*, Czytelnik, 1956, but not in subsequent editions.

the face on tribute money: Caesar's, as recounted in Matthew 22 when Jesus is shown a coin by a Pharisee.

"Reed": Sent to Henryk Elzenberg in a letter dated November 17, 1951; first published in Zbigniew Herbert and Henryk Elzenberg, *Korespondencja* (Correspondence), ed. B. Toruńczyk, Warsaw: Fundacja Zeszytów Literackich, 2002.

"Roll Call": Published in ". . . I must choose every moment," in *An Almanac of Poetry*. Warsaw, PAX, 1954.

"Composition with Birds": Published in ". . . I must choose every moment," in *An Almanac of Poetry*. Warsaw, PAX, 1954.

"To Flora (Eclogue)": Published in Z. Herbert, *Utwory rozproszone.* (Uncollected Works. Reconnaissance; hereafter ZHUR), ed. R. Krynicki, Krakow: a5 Press, 2010.

"Litany to Irony": Transcribed from manuscript by R. Krynicki and published in *Kwartalnik Artystyczny*, no. 87, 2015.

"Nikifor": Published in *Tygodnik Powszechny*, no. 41, October 1957, along with a review by Herbert (signed "Patryk") of a book about Nikifor by Andrzej Banach, *Nikifor mistrz z Krynicy*.

"Lovers": Published in *Mazury i Warmia*, no. 6, July 1956.

"On the Repatriation of Bruno Jasieński's Remains": Published in ZHUR. Bruno Jasieński, born Wiktor Bruno Zysman (1901–1938), Polish poet and leader of the Futurist movement in the interbellum; author of *I Burn Paris* (1928). Executed during Stalin's Great Purge and rehabilitated in 1955.

"Night": Published in *Znak*, no. 1, January 1958.

"On the Necessity of Schooling": Published in *Życie Literackie*, no. 3, January 1957.

"My Star": Published in *Znak*, no. 1, January 1958.

"Little Lament": Published in *Twórczość*, no. 2, February 1958.

"Deceased": Poem included in the text of the play for voices *Lalek*; the title derives from an archive draft.

"Little Town": Poem included in the text of the play for voices *Lalek*. The Herbert archive holds a significant variant of the poem:

> A little town
> bolted and locked
> with the azure key
> of a lake
>
> I could live here
> as if in a broken clock
> in the middle of the sky
>
> the only memorial
> that survived here
> a stoic goat
> in the middle of the market
>
> from the froth of dawn
> up to the froth of death

it runs on its own
no one winds it up

even a photographer
the only historian
praises children
and newlyweds

I could stay here
if it weren't for that driveway
paved
with Jewish gravestones

"Grove": Published in *Odra*, no. 13, April 1958.

"Box": Published in *Odra*, no. 13, April 1958.

"Funeral of a Hippopotamus": Published in *Odra*, no. 13, April 1958.

"Colantonio—S. Gierolamo e il leone": Published in *Litery*, no. 7, July 1971; originally included in a letter to Jerzy Zawieyski, January 4, 1960. The dedication was added in 1971.

****"the mountains finally turned": Published in *Wiersze* (Poems), London, 1964, a samizdat edition printed by Magdalena and Zbigniew Czajkowski. Later included in the German selection *Inschrift* (translation by K. Dedecius, Frankfurt, 1967).

****"under a tree without color": Published in *Wiersze* (Poems), London, 1964.

****"the evening city": Published in *Wiersze* (Poems), London, 1964.

****"nightingales on the Île St-Louis start up in mid-March": Published in *Wiersze* (Poems), London 1964.

****"In a clearing under a tree Johann Kaspar Lavater waited": Published in *Współczesność*, no. 11, 1961.

"Hair": Published in *Współczesność*, no. 11, 1961.

"From Herodotus": Transcribed from corrected MS in folder Study of the Object in Herbert archive; dated "Athens, October 5, 1964"; first published in ZHUR.

"Mr Cogito and Certain Mechanisms of Memory": Published in ZHUR.

"Mycenae": Published in *Zeszyty Literackie*, no. 4, 1999, and subsequently in "Kochane Zwierzatka," letters by Zbigniew Herbert to his friends Magdalena and Zbigniew Czajkowski. Warsaw, 2000.

"Words": Published in ZHUR.

****"during a sleepless night": Published in ZHUR.

"Mr Cogito's Addendum to the Tragedy of Mayerling": Published first in German translation, by Karl Dedecius, in *Herr Cogito*. First Polish publication in *Kwartalnik Artystyczny*, no. 2, 2000.

"Mr Cogito and the Tasks of Art": Published in *Kwartalnik Artystyczny*, no. 87, 2015.

"Angels of Civilization": Published first in German translation, by Karl Dedecius, in *Herr Cogito*. Gedichte. In Polish in Zbigniew Herbert, *Wiersze wybrane* (Selected Poems).

"Cat (II)": Published first in German translation, by Karl Dedecius, in *Herr Cogito*. In Polish in Zbigniew Herbert, *Wiersze wybrane* (Selected Poems).

"Knot": Published first in German translation, by Karl Dedecius, in *Herr Cogito*. In Polish in Zbigniew Herbert, *Wiersze wybrane* (Selected Poems).

"Monomakh's Cap": Published in German translation in Herbert, *Herr Cogito*, Frankfurt am Main, 1974. First Polish publication in *Zeszyty Literackie*, no. 4/68, 1999.

"Mr Cogito's Dream": Published in German translation in Herbert, *Herr Cogito*, Frankfurt am Main, 1974.

> *Amphitheatrum Sapientiae Aeternae*: Amphitheater of Eternal Knowledge, an alchemical treatise by the German doctor, alchemist, and cabalist Heinrich Khunrath (1560–1605), published in Hamburg in 1595.

"Mr Cogito's Dream-Awakening": Published in German translation in Herbert, *Herr Cogito*, Frankfurt am Main, 1974. First Polish publication in *Zeszyty Literackie*, no. 4/68, 1999.

"From Mr Cogito's Erotica": Published in German in *Akzente*, no. 2, 1975. First Polish publication in *Zeszyty Literackie*, no. 4/68, 1999.

"From the Firm's History (June 1976)": Published in *Tygodnik Solidarność*, no. 13, 1981.

"From an Unwritten Theory of Dreams (In memory of Jean Améry)": Published in ZHUR, transcribed from manuscript drafts.

> *Jean Améry*: Austrian writer born as Hans Chaim Mayer in Vienna in 1912; one of Herbert's most deeply valued friends. Mayer emigrated to Belgium in 1938 and underwent repeated imprisonment in camps in France and Belgium (where he was severely tortured) and, after 1943, in Auschwitz, Buchenwald, and Bergen-Belsen. After liberation he lived in Brussels as an independent writer, publishing the 1966 essay collection "Jenseits von Schuld und Sühne. Bewältigungsversuche eines Uberwältigten" (Beyond Guilt and Penance. Attempts to Overcome by One Overcome, published in English as "At the Mind's Limits: Contemplations by a Survivor on Auschwitz and Its Realities"), as well as essays on many subjects including jazz, aging, and suicide. He took his own life in October 1978.

"Generation": Published in ZHUR, transcribed from manuscript drafts.

> The poets seen here as members of one generation are Paul Celan (born 1920), Ingeborg Bachmann (1926), Marian Ośniałowski (1920), John Berryman (1914), Sylvia Plath (1932), Günter Bruno Fuchs (1928), Tadeusz Kazimerz Sułkowski (1907), János Pilinszky (1921).

"Our Child": Published in *Tygodnik Powszechny*, no. 14, 1980.

"Sleep's Decorations": Published in ZHUR.

****"my poor kingdom I still defend you": Published in *Kwartalnik Artystyczny*, no. 93, 2017.

"On the Day of Judgment": Published in ZHUR. Archive draft is undated but probably derives from the late 1970s.

"Mr Cogito and Utopias": Published in ZHUR.

****"That little hand on the white sheet": Published in *Zeszyty Literackie*, no. 32, 1990. In a note to the editor Barbara Toruńczyk, Herbert wrote: "I enclose a little poem which I myself find odd."

"Contra Augustinum Pontificem in Terra Nubica Peccatorem in Purgatorio": Published in *Zeszyty Literackie*, no. 4, 1999. The archive manuscript is marked "Ferrara 20/21 X 1990."

> The Latin title translates as "Against Augustine, priest in Nubian land, sinner in Purgatory."
>
> *ama et fac quod vis*: love and do what you will, a paraphrase of Augustine, "dilige et quod vis fac," from *In Joannis Evangelium Tractatus* (VII 8).

"A Stone in Jerusalem": Published in *Kwartalnik Artystyczny*, no. 79, 2013.

    Herbert refers to David Weinfeld, his Israeli translator, and to Yehuda Amichai and Dan Pagis, Israeli poets. In his notes to this poem in ZHUR 2, Ryszard Krynicki indicates the probability of "Al" being a reference to Aleksander Schenker, to whom ZH dedicated the poem "Mitteleuropa" in *Rovigo*; another possibility is Al Alvarez, the British critic and champion of Herbert's work; Peter Rühmkorf (1929–2008) was a German poet.

****"I'm looking for the poems of Dan Pagis": Published in *Kwartalnik Artystyczny*, no. 2, 2009.

"Trenches": Published in ZHUR.

"To Michael Krüger": Published in *Kwartalnik Artystyczny*, no. 84, 2014.

"Mr Cogito's Disability": Published in ZHUR 2.

"Epilogue to the Tempest": Published in *Zeszyty Literackie*, no. 2/70, 2000.

"The Reality of Evil": Published in ZHUR 2.

"Mandelstam": Published in ZHUR.

    As Ryszard Krynicki writes in a note to this poem, which seems to have arisen in 1991, it exists in three draft versions, all difficult to decipher. One is titled "Taniec" (Dance):

> [raucous applause of the zeks]
> And Mandelstam dances amid the hearty cries of the zeks
> who magnanimously pelt his face with apple cores
> he dances like Socrates almost naked now a knee now an elbow blossoms
> from his rags enhancing the comical effect of a ballet of despair
> What is his dance about obviously about terror the terror of the body
> that does not want to suffer and the spirit as if it lived on its own
> on a high cliff over the tempestuous bay when it comes in with full tide
> And Mandelstam dances like a Hasid in ecstasy
> throws up his arms gives out harrowing wails and whines
> the zeks are beside themselves with joy
> And Mandelstam dances barefoot on the snow alone

"Spring": Published in ZHUR.

"Winter": Published in *Zeszyty Literackie*, no. 4/68 1999.

"Hagiographic-Zoological Meditations of Mr Cogito": Published in *Kwartalnik Artystyczny*, no. 85, 2015.

"Breviary. Trifles": Published in *Zeszyty Literackie*, no. 4/72, 2000.

"Untitled (for Barbara Toruńczyk)": Published in *Zeszyty Literackie*, no. 4/68, 1999.

"Miron": Published in *Kwartalnik Artystyczny*, no. 96, 2017.

    Ryszard Krynicki: "It is worth noting that in 1956 ZH wrote an article titled 'Ślepi przechodnie' (Blind Passersby) about Miron Białoszewski's poetry and private experimental theater, Teatr na Tarczynskiej." Unpublished in his lifetime, the piece appeared in *Zeszyty Literackie*, no. 106, 2/2009, and is reprinted in ZHUR.

"End": Published in *Zeszyty Literackie*, no. 4/68, 1999.

"Conversation": Published in ZHUR.